THE 1.

VOLUME ONE

To Judge or Not to Judge

KENNETH WAPNICK, Ph.D.

Foundation for A COURSE IN MIRACLES®

Foundation for A COURSE IN MIRACLES®
375 N Stephanie St, Suite 2311
Henderson, NV 89014
www.facim.org

Copyright 2022 by the
Foundation for A COURSE IN MIRACLES®

Printed in the United States of America

First printing, 2022

Portions of *A Course in Miracles* © 1975, 1992
Psychotherapy: Purpose, Process and Practice © 1976, 2004
The Gifts of God © 1982
used by permission of the Foundation for Inner Peace.

ISBN 978-1-59142-944-9

Introduction
Judgment and the Authority Problem

The title of the workshop, "To Judge or Not to Judge" is obviously taken from the famous line from Hamlet, "To be or not to be." Unfortunately, this is not what the right question is, because as we will be talking about later on, we cannot avoid judging. And the real question is not whether we judge or do not judge, but with whom do we make our judgments. Do we make them with the ego or the Holy Spirit?

I think one of the confusions many students of the Course have is in thinking that when the Course says not to judge, it means not to make judgments such as what I am going to eat tonight, or what color suit or dress I am going to put on, or where I am going to spend my weekend or with whom. That is not what the Course is talking about. What it means, again, by not judging, is not to condemn and not to attack. Clearly, if the Holy Spirit is our guide in judgment, then what we judge will not be an attack. And when the Holy Spirit is not our guide and the ego is our guide, which really are the only choices open to us, then it must be an attack. And we will spend a lot of time this weekend talking about that.

I just wanted to begin by reading a couple of lines from the text, page 47. It is the second paragraph. Judgment is perhaps one of the most important concepts that the Course addresses. One of the characteristics of God's teachers is tolerance (M-4.III). In the discussion of tolerance, it is really talking about not judging. And this passage I am going to read from now makes that very clear.

(T.3.VI.3:1) You have no idea of the tremendous release and deep peace that comes from meeting yourself and your brothers totally without judgment.

"Without judgment" here means without seeing someone else as separate, without attacking or condemning. I think that this line is extremely important to always keep in mind. It is

Jesus' way of reminding us that we have no idea of the gain to us when we are able to give up our judgments and our attack thoughts. If we are truly serious about finding the peace of God, then the only way we can find that peace and experience that peace and His love is to give up judgment. In effect, we could say that the whole *Course in Miracles*, one of its major purposes, is to show us first how we are judging all the time, and not judging with love; and then to give us the means whereby we can change our minds about these judgments.

(T.3.VI.3:2-3) When you recognize what you are and what your brothers are, [which is really that we are all part of the same Christ] **you will realize that judging them in any way is without meaning. In fact, their meaning is lost to you precisely *because* you are judging them.**

We will see in just a minute as I discuss the origin of judgment, that the whole purpose and motivation in back of our judgments and holding onto grievances and choosing right from wrong and dividing up the world into good versus evil, etc., etc., the whole motivation in that is precisely to keep the true meaning of ourselves hidden from us. And that meaning is that we are all one in Christ. That remembrance is what the Course refers to as the Atonement principle; namely, that the separation from God never truly happened.

Our judgments are not something that occur to us or that spontaneously arise in our minds. Rather, our judgments are things that we choose specifically to further our identity with the ego and to attack the Holy Spirit's love in our mind, again, which is a love that sees all people as being one.

The Origin of Judgment

What I would like to do first is to go over the origin of judgment and then show how all the little judgments that we make in our daily living are nothing more than a reflection of that original judgment, which really is just another way of talking about our separation from God. But I would like to discuss that from the point of view of judgment. Another way of understanding what judgment is, is that all judgment is based upon differences. Now this is one of the key ideas, not only in understanding judgment, which is what we will be talking about this weekend, but also in understanding special relationships, which is the epitome of the ego's judgment. Without a belief in differences, there would be no special relationships and there'd be no separation.

And we can understand the origin of the separation as being that instant, which the Course refers to as the tiny, mad idea (T-27.VIII.6:2). It is that instant when the thought of separation crept into the mind of God's Son. In that instant, which the Course explains never truly happened, but which seemed to happen, we made the first judgment. And that judgment was that there is a difference between God, Who's the Creator, and the Son of God, who is the created.

Before that thought seemed to arise, there was no difference, or certainly there was no perception of difference and there was no experience of difference. The Course does explain that indeed, there is a difference between God and Christ; namely, God is the Creator and Christ is the created. But there is no separated consciousness or duality consciousness that can perceive such a difference. The Course explains that there is no place where the Father ends and the Son begins (W-pI.132.12:4). There is a difference in the sense, again, that God is the Creator, God is the Source, God is the First Cause. And His Son Christ is the effect, the created.

But once again, Christ does not have a separated mind or a separated consciousness that can observe this difference or experience this difference. One of the ways of understanding what Heaven is, is that it's the awareness of perfect Oneness. That the state of Heaven, the state of being in Heaven is the perfect unity of God and Christ. And it's a unity that can never be separated, broken, fragmented. etc.

When the tiny, mad idea seemed to arise—again, that thought of being separate—what resulted was the Son of God now appeared to be separate from his Creator, and now had a consciousness that was separate from the Consciousness or the Mind of God. Where before there was the Mind of God and the Mind of Christ that were perfectly One, now there is the Mind of God and the Mind of Christ, which are perfectly One, and what appears to be a split mind, which appears to be separate from its Source.

Once again, the original separation thought is that instant when the Son of God perceived a difference between himself and God and from that moment, he then made the judgment that God has something that I don't have. And that is the original judgment. It is a judgment or perception of lack within the Sonship that says there is something missing. And what is wrong here is that God created me; I did not create Him.

Now again as we have seen, that is a Fact in Heaven. In fact, the Course would spell that with a capital "F"—that God created Christ and Christ did not create God. But once again, there is no awareness of that. There is no difference, there is no perception, there is no judgment. But once the separation began, which as the Course explains in other places is the beginning of the dream, there is the perception of differences and that automatically leads to a perception, which is a judgment, that God has something I don't have and there is something wrong with that; that's not fair.

Again, God has what I don't have; namely, He is the Creator and I am not. He has the power to create me; I lack that power. I cannot create Him. We could say then that the original judgment and therefore all subsequent judgments, as we will elaborate on in a little while, begin with the perception of difference, which leads to the perception of lack. There is something wrong with me; there is something missing inside of me. And so once again, that is the original judgment. God has something I don't have.

4

What then follows inevitably and all within one instant is the total unfolding of the ego thought system. What inevitably follows from the perception of lack, which the Course at one point (Preface) calls the "scarcity principle," which basically is another word for guilt. There is something wrong with me, that there is something missing in me. From that perception of scarcity and lack inevitably arises the projection of the responsibility for that. The reason I am lacking something is because God took it from me. In other words, that I am deprived of the power to create life.

We could say that the belief in scarcity inevitably becomes projected out and leads to the belief in deprivation. Somebody else did this to me. I began with a judgment that there was something wrong with myself. It now evolves into the judgment, somebody took this from me. It's somebody else's fault that I am not the First Cause. Since at that point in the story, there is no one else on the scene except God, then obviously God must be the guilty one.

Rather than it was myself who was lacking, which was the initial judgment that I made and therefore is the initial judgment that we all make in our experiences here, I now transfer the responsibility for that lack and I place it onto God. I say it was really God Who lacked in the beginning, because I had it and He took it from me. And therefore, I am now justified in taking it back from Him. That is the original theft, which in Greek mythology you find in the Prometheus story, who steals fire from Zeus. And then of course Zeus goes after him, eventually captures him and metes out a cruel punishment to him.

The theft that we believe we are actually accomplishing is to steal from God this creative power. And I feel justified in doing so because in my warped mind, in my insanity, which is the core of the dream, I believe that God had done it to me first. Therefore, I am justified in stealing from Him. But what inevitably follows from that, which we won't spend a lot of time on this weekend, is that we then believe God is going to come after us and is going to try to punish us and steal back from us what we stole from Him, because we believe God stole it from us first. That is the origin of our fear of God. And that is the origin of the judgment that God is not our friend; God is our enemy.

What gets set up in this, which once again is the basis for all the subsequent judgments that we have ever made, are making now or will ever make is the judgment that this world is divided up into victims and victimizers. Obviously, we all believe that we are the innocent victims and other people are victimizing us. That is the core of all the judgments that we make. Underneath that, of course, is the horrible truth that we never want to look at, which is that I am not the innocent victim; I am the original victimizer. And I am the one who has stolen. But what the ego does is blot that out so we forget that. Rather it becomes that we are the innocent victims and other people are trying to steal from us what is rightfully ours.

This is the basic thought that underlies everyone's mind; again, namely this judgment of God and His Son being different, that we were the ones who victimized God. We then believe God is going to victimize us. And again, those are the original judgments. These thoughts are absolutely terrifying, because what we are talking about is a sense of sin and a sense of guilt that is woven into the very fabric of our being. That is the basic substance of the split mind—that there is in fact a difference.

I know there is a difference because I am here and God is outside of me. That there is the mind of my self and then there is the Mind of God. And it's that Mind of God that has become the enemy. That is the basic split that we all share, and the terror that rises from that. The defense that we all have employed to escape from that awesome guilt and the terror of God's destruction is that we blot the whole thing from our mind, we deny that the whole thing ever happened, and we then run and hide and make up a world, which we believe will protect us from God's fury and God's wrath, or from God's judgment of us.

We can begin to see here the origin of all of the wrath of God passages that we grew up with, whether we grew up a Jew or Christian. The thought that God is going to pursue us and punish us and destroy the world, and save some people and punish the rest—all that comes from this original thought that God and His Son are different and God is angry. God is justified in being angry because of what we have done to Him, and that we have to run and hide. This world, as the Course explains, then becomes this huge hiding place in which we believe God can never enter.

"Ideas Leave Not Their Source"

One of the key principles in the Course is the thought that "ideas leave not their source" (T-26.VII.4:7,13:2). This is one of the most important principles to understand because it underlies not only what the Atonement principle is, which is the Holy Spirit's thought, but also underlies everything in the ego system. The idea that "ideas leave not their source" connotes is that we are all ideas in the Mind of God. We are all Thoughts in His Mind, spelled with a capital "T." If ideas leave not their source, then the idea of God's Son, the idea of Christ, can never leave his Source in his Father. That basically again would be what the Atonement principle is—that the separation never happened because the Son never left his Father.

The ego's principle, of course, is just the opposite—that ideas do leave their source. And that the idea of God's Son can indeed leave his Source, be separate from his Creator and establish a self and a world and a kingdom that is independent and separate from that of God. That same principle also works within the split mind itself, within this world. If ideas leave not their source, and the world is seen as an idea, which is one of the central themes of the Course, it is an idea then that has also never left its source, which is in the Son's mind.

Which means despite the fact that there appears to be a world outside of us, the truth of it is all that we are seeing is a projection of our own thoughts, and we have forgotten that we projected it. In the same way as when we are sitting in front of a movie and are thoroughly engrossed in what is on the screen, then we become so identified with the characters that we are observing and the situations that are being depicted, that we totally forget in that moment or series of moments that we are engrossed in what is going on in the movie—we forget that this is actually make-believe. There are no real people on the screen. There are not people who are living or dying or are being hurt or falling in love and living happily ever after, or people who are separated and people who are in misery.

The very fact that we find a movie as a relaxation or something to get our minds off our troubles is witness to the fact of how the mind can so easily deny what, on another level, it knows is true. Everyone knows that nothing goes on on the screen, that it literally is all make-believe. That doesn't stop us, however, from having all the emotions, feelings and thoughts that we have in what we think of as our ongoing, waking, regular life. We will be happy, we will be sad, we will be anxious, we will be terrified, we will be guilty, we will be depressed, we will be bored, etc., etc., etc.

The reason all this works is again because of the mechanism of denial. We forget where the movie is coming from. It is really not outside of us; it's really coming from in back of us. It is really coming from a film that is running through a projector and it's all made up. Real people are not on the screen.

The relationship of this external world to our mind is exactly the same, except when we leave a movie theater, we walk outside and we remember then that it was all made up. When we awaken from a dream at night, we remember that it was a dream and not "reality"—"reality" in quotes, of course. But in this world, it appears as if we don't awaken from the dream and we never leave the movie theater. Because we really do believe there is a world outside of us. And that is because we have forgotten, through the mechanism of denial, repression, that we are the ones who have made it up.

So once again, the principle that ideas leave not their source is saying that the idea of a separated world has never left its source, which is in the mind. Which is the Course's way of explaining why there is no world, or certainly there is no world out there. There is a belief in a world, there is an experience of a world, but there is no world outside of us (W-pI.132.6:2). But it's essential, if the ego is going to survive, that it continually convince us there is a world outside in which there are victims and victimizers outside, in which there are judgments that are justified outside.

So we never go back into our mind, which the ego tells us, if we ever do, we would be destroyed by God's wrath. Of course, what the ego never tells us is that if we do return to our mind, we will not find this awful, awesome, horrifying wrath of God. What we will find is His gentle and accepting love. And that in fact nothing has happened. This is all nothing more than a bad dream.

Rather than have us experience that this is nothing more than a dream, because that means the end of the ego, the ego then pulls the wool over our eyes, or pulls the world over our eyes, so that we believe there is something outside of us. Then it makes up bodies, which bring our brain sensory data, which our brain then interprets for us that indeed proves to us that there is indeed a world outside. And we will read a workbook lesson a little while later, which explains this.

The purpose of the body, which really is a microcosm of the world's purpose, is to continually prove to us there is something outside to which we should pay attention. Because if I pay attention to what is outside, once again, I am not paying attention to what is inside. That is my ego's fear. If I pay attention to what is inside, I will not be destroyed by an angry, wrathful God. I'll simply be welcomed back to the God of love Whom I never really left.

In order to preserve its identity as a split mind and as a sinful, fearful thought, what the ego does is continually have our attention be focused outside of us. Judgment, as we will see in just a minute, becomes one of the crucial ways in which the ego does this. Because all judgment is based upon differences, by definition virtually, because I cannot judge between something unless there is a difference between them. I cannot judge between two people whom I want to see or two pairs of pants that I want to put on or two events that I want to attend, unless I recognize that there is a difference, and that I know which difference or which thing, which event, which pair of clothes, which person, is better for me to choose.

All of our judgments in the world are based upon differences. As long as we can keep that in mind always and remember the origin of that judgment, then we can see very clearly how all of this is just a very subtle and yet very clever trick of the ego. That is why in one of the passages on time, which is one of the central ploys of the ego, the Course talks about time as being a magic trick, a sleight of hand (W-pI.158.4:1). That really is just a symbol for what the ego is. The ego is a super magician. Because as long as I make judgments in the world and believe those judgments are justified and are real and are valid, what I am doing is reinforcing the original judgment, that there is a difference between God and myself. If there is indeed a difference between God and His Son, of which I am a part, then it means the separation thought is real, which means that the ego is alive and well.

Moreover, it means that the Holy Spirit is a liar, because the Holy Spirit is always telling us—He told us right in that original instant, and therefore is telling us all throughout our day and all of our experiences—that the Atonement principle is true; namely, the separation never happened. Not only did it not happen between myself and my Creator, but it also has not happened between myself and you. All of my judgments upon you that you are different from me, that you have something that I do not have, are all part of the ego dream.

The Atonement principle, again, is that the separation never truly happened, which means that not only should we not make judgments, but that as the Course explains at one point, that we cannot make judgments. We can believe we can judge. We believe within our experience in this world as a split mind, as an ego, that we can judge. But in truth, all that judgment is, is part of the dream. We can no more judge a difference between ourselves and God than we could to acknowledge that we are separate from God. All judgment, then, is simply part and parcel and integrated into the very fabric of the ego thought system. Without judgment, you have no ego.

Basically, we will see that God doesn't judge. And we will see near the end of the workshop, when we discuss what the Course refers to as God's final judgment, that it's not using the word "judgment" as we usually think of it. God's judgment on us is what it always was and what it could never change—and that simply is that we are His beloved Son. Love has never been broken, it's never been separated and can never be judged against.

The belief that we can judge is the belief that God can be destroyed, that God can be fragmented. Because you cannot have a state of unified awareness and judge. Judgment again automatically means I am judging between two options. It is not only that I am seeing a difference between option A and option B, but I believe that I am separate from option A and option B and that I can choose between them.

Smiling at Our Judgments

Q: To illustrate the principles that you've been talking about, could we use the example of the typical driving situation where I am on the entrance ramp to the parkway and the first car that comes along cuts me off and won't let me in. And then the second car that comes along lets me in. Now how would I process this without judging the first driver as the bad guy and the second driver as the good guy?

A: What you do, which is something that we will discuss again later on in the weekend, is you just say, "Oh, I am judging again. What else is new?" I still believe that judging is going to keep me away from God's punishment. I realize now, because I am such a good *Course in Miracles* student, that all that judgment is going to do is keep me away from God's Love, which must mean I am still afraid of God's Love, which means, as Jesus is constantly telling me in the Course, I am still partially insane. I knew that anyway. In other words, you don't make a big deal about the judgment. And when you can learn not to make a big deal about judgment, whether it's your judgments about somebody else or another person's judgments about you or about another person, then that is a major step in learning not to take that tiny, mad idea (the original judgment) seriously.

Q: The Course would say if I use this thought system, then the next morning when that same thing happened, I probably won't be as upset?

A: You probably won't be as upset, that's right. If you don't take it seriously. But if you fight against it, and you stop your car and get out and do your workbook lesson furiously (laughter) the chances are you are going to have to do it a lot. What you want to do is just learn how to smile at the judgment. We will see a bit later on in the workshop, again, that in that original instant, when the ego made that judgment, it made that judgment extremely serious.

It said that this difference that I perceive between God and myself is sinful. And either it becomes I sinned against God, or I then project it out and believe God has sinned against me. And it's from that sin that I feel guilty, and that I am terrified. The whole thing has suddenly become very, very serious.

What the Holy Spirit does is simply say isn't that a silly thought, that you could be different from your Creator? That you could exist outside of your Source. The way that we regain that original thought of the Holy Spirit, "That this is silly," is to watch all the judgments that we make, from the time that we wake up in the morning. You start driving your car and something like you described happens. You say, "Oh, I am doing it again. Isn't that silly?' I really believe making this judgment against this driver or making this judgment against this person, or holding onto this grievance, is going to keep God's Love away from me.

And that is what I want—to keep God's Love away from me. "Isn't that silly?" First, it's silly to believe that I can keep God's Love away from me, because God's Love is within me. I can't keep it away from me. What I can do is I can keep it away from my experience or awareness. That I can do. But I can't keep it away from me. And isn't it silly for me to even want to keep it away from me? And that is what we do. And then go right on being angry.

Q: So you don't make the error real?

A: You don't make the error real.

All things are echoes of the Voice for God

I want to look at workbook lesson 151. It's the lesson that is entitled, "All things are echoes of the Voice for God." The Voice for God, of course is the Holy Spirit. It's lesson 151 in the workbook, which is page 278. "All things are echoes of the Voice for God." Let me explain a little bit about what this lesson is about first. Then we will read through a lot of it. As I mentioned briefly earlier, the purpose of the world and the purpose of the body is to keep the guilt and the fear of our mind hidden from us, which in turn serves to keep the love of God hidden from us.

The ego tells us that what it's going to protect us from is our guilt and our fear. What it doesn't tell us is that what it's really trying to protect us from, which is really what it is trying to protect itself from, is the love of God. The belief in the ego, the belief in sin, the belief in guilt, the belief in fear, the belief in attack, etc., are all different forms of the original judgment, once again, that says that God and myself, God and His son, are different. So that once again, differences and judgments are what keep the ego thought system alive. That is extremely important.

This whole world, then, was based upon a judgment. The judgment being that I have separated from God. God is angry at me. He's going to punish me. So this world then has to save me. But once again, it's the ego thought of judgment that is the thought system that we have become, we have identified with. And that therefore, since ideas leave not their source, it's the thought system that is reflected in this world.

It is not possible that what we see on the movie screen in front of us be any different from what the film is that is running through the film projector. Whatever that film is that is running through the projector must be identical to what we are perceiving on the screen, because ideas leave not their source. What is outside must be what is inside. What is inside must be projected outside.

What is inside the mind of each of us is this judgment, this original judgment that we are separate and different from God. Since that is the underlying thought, and it's that thought that therefore will be projected out and make the world, then this therefore must be a world of judgment. The purpose of the body is to make judgments.

As the Course explains in greater detail in the text, but it's going to talk about it here in this lesson now, the body, which is ruled by the brain, which is part of the body, was made to carry out the wishes and to express in form the thought that is within the mind. Remember again, ideas leave not their source. What is in the mind, which is the source, must express itself in the idea of form, the idea of the world, the idea of a body. So what I perceive outside is exactly what I am perceiving inside.

If I perceive separation inside and guilt and attack and defense and victim and victimizer inside, I must perceive that outside. It is my body, once again, that makes that perception real for me. If I had no body, then I wouldn't know about it. That is why the ego mind makes up a body, so that it can prove that the separation is real, but that it's real outside of me. And my body is outside of me. Because the "me" that I am talking about, just as the "you" that Jesus is always addressing in the Course, is the mind, not the body.

So the body is outside of me, just as the world is outside of me. The ego would have me believe that separation and differences and judgments are real, but they are outside of my mind and not within my mind, because the ego doesn't want me anywhere near my mind, because that is where the love of God is, and that is what the ego is afraid of. So that is the purpose of the body and the world.

What the mind then does is to essentially serve as a computer programmer, that programs the computer, which is the brain. It tells the brain and the body what to perceive, what to judge. And just as the computer that is totally dumb and cannot think unless a programmer puts a program in—that is exactly what the body and the brain are. They are totally dumb. They don't do anything; they don't think, they don't act.

As the Course explains, they are not born, they don't die; bodies don't get sick, bodies don't get well. They simply carry out what the programmer tells them to do. And the programmer is the mind. It is the mind that programs the body and the brain to make judgments, because that is what the mind consists of—one big judgment—God and His Son are different. Not only are they different, but they are at war with each other.

But once again, the ego doesn't want me to see that battlefield within me, it wants me to perceive the battlefield outside of me. I believe the war is being waged between bodies out here, whether we are talking about one country fighting another country or one religion fighting another religion, one sports team fighting another sports team, or all the kinds of special relationships that go on in our life where we feel we are at war with everybody else. The purpose of all of these is to convince us the battle is outside, that it has to be won outside, that there is going to be a winner and a loser. Someone who will be victorious, another who will be defeated. So I don't go back within where the original judgment is so I can look at it.

The reason behind the point I was making earlier, that you don't judge against your judgments; you simply look at them—is that the problem was that we never looked at the original judgment. If we had looked at the original judgment that we had made, saying that, "I have indeed stolen from God and separated from Him," and really looked at it, I would have realized how preposterous it was, and how silly it was to believe that a part of God could wrench away from Him, let alone steal His power and then declare itself as God. That is absolutely insane. It makes no sense at all.

But I never looked at it. None of us ever looked at it. We know that we never looked at it because we are here. The very fact that we are here is saying that we believe in a sinful, guilty, separated self. The ego never wants us to look at that original judgment. Instead what it does is that it takes the judgment, which is within our mind, and it projects it out. We now make all the judgments to our heart's content that are external. One body judges against another body.

We believe that we are justified and our judgments are valid. Your judgments against me are not valid, but mine against you are valid. The judgments my country makes against your country are valid, but not vice versa. We are convinced that we are right and someone else is wrong. That is why, near the end of the text, Jesus asks, "Do you prefer that you be right or happy?" (T-29.VII.1:9). We all want to be right. Because that is what we asserted to God right at the beginning, "I am right and you are wrong." That is what we asserted to the Holy Spirit right at the beginning, "I am right and you are wrong." There is a difference between us. My judgment against you is valid. We are separate. And what you are teaching me is not true. Our original judgment, then, is perceived as real and is then never looked at again.

Instead, the ego, which is the mind, which is the programmer, makes up a world and a body, and programs the brain to see judgment, differences and separation as real and as outside of us. Therefore, we believe what our bodies' eyes, our bodies' ears, our sense of smell and touch, etc.—our senses tell us is outside of us is true and is real. Now on one level, of course, the Course is not asking us to deny what we judge in the world. That is what I mentioned right at the beginning, that we can't help making judgments here.

But we can help and begin to change our mind about the judgments we make about each other. In a world of the body, which is what we all exist in, and again, we are not asked ever to deny our physical experience in the world. There is a passage early on in the text where Jesus says that it's practically impossible to deny one's physical experience in the world (T-2.IV.3:10). We are not asked to avoid making judgments as we go through our daily life. Again, we are asked to avoid making judgments that attack and condemn and exclude.

(W-pI.151.1:1-2) No one can judge on partial evidence. That is not judgment.

What this is saying is that the only meaningful judgment anyone can make is when you know all the facts. The Course explains here and in several other places, there is no way we can make any accurate judgment, because we don't have all the facts, because our bodies and our brains were made to keep the true facts away from us. Because the true Fact is that God is the only Fact and everything else is a defense and an illusion that we put against Him. We basically judge on partial evidence. We only judge what our egos would have us see.

(W-pI.151.1:2-3) That is not judgment. It is merely an opinion based on ignorance and doubt.

The ignorance is that we are totally ignorant of what is truth, because truth is the Holy Spirit's presence in our mind. And we doubt because we doubt ourselves; we doubt who we really are.

(W-pI.151.1:4) Its seeming certainty is but a cloak for the uncertainty it would conceal.

This is extremely important. Everybody is certain about what we perceive. Everybody in this room, if we counted, would come up with the same number of people here. Everybody would look outside and say it is nighttime rather than daytime. And we'd be absolutely certain we were correct. Just to take it down to the individual level, we are absolutely certain about what we believe. We are absolutely certain that we are right and other people are wrong. We are absolutely certain that our judgments are right and other people's judgments are wrong.

We do that both on the psychological level as well as on the gross physical level, where we are certain about what it is that we perceive and think. Yet all of this is simply a defense against what is really uncertain in our mind. The uncertainty in our mind is the ego, which rests upon a very uncertain premise, which is the premise that the separation from God is real. Because the certainty is what the Atonement principle is; namely, that the separation is not real. What is uncertain is that the separation and the judgments we have made against ourselves and God are real. But in truth, that is uncertain, because it rests upon a lie. And yet what we do, the ego never has us look within our mind to see that uncertainty and that lie. Rather what we do is cover it over and make up a world and make up a body and a brain that perceives the world. We now become certain about what reality is, and about what truth is.

One of the major advances, I think, of this century is quantum physics, which is helping us recognize within the hard-core science of physics that the world we perceive is not really there. And that what we are so certain about is an illusion. It is simply a product of our thought. And that we can never objectively look at or study or understand anything that is outside of us. I think that is extremely important because it's a very helpful way of breaking down the certainty we all have about what appears to be the reality of the outside world.

Newtonian physics was a physics and a science that was based upon certainty. If we studied and learned and observed and analyzed long enough, we would understand everything in the universe and be able to predict and control everything. And because our perceptions would be certain, our data would be certain, our conclusions would be certain. What the new physics has taught us is that we can't be certain about anything.

(W-pI.151.1:5) It needs irrational defense because it is irrational.

The uncertainty is irrational, which literally means non-rational or non-reason. The Course uses the word "reason" as a synonym for right-minded thinking or the Holy Spirit's thinking. That is what reason is. What is non-reason or irrational is the ego's thought system. And because it's irrational then, it needs a defense to protect it, which must also be irrational, which is this world. If ideas leave not their source, and the source of the world is the irrational and uncertain idea that we are separate from God, then the world must also be irrational and uncertain. Because, again, ideas leave not their source.

But the body was made to protect that irrationality from ever being looked at. What the body does is tell us, "Yes, indeed, there is a rational world out there and I can be certain about what I see." I forget that I am only certain about what I see because I was programmed that way. I was programmed really to make the irrational rational and to make the illusory true. To make what is love into something that is fearful. And I am sure that I am right. Another way of saying this, is that I am sure that my judgments are right. They are *my* judgments. And the judgments are based upon who I am as a separated self. And those judgments are held to be true while the judgment of the Holy Spirit is held to be false.

(W-pI.151.1:6) And its defense [which would be the whole thought system of the ego, which ends up with the body and the world] **seems strong, convincing, and without a doubt because of all the doubting underneath.**

This is true for all of us whether you are talking about someone who is psychotic or not. A psychotic is filled, from a psychological point of view, with tremendous self-doubt and tremendous terror and tremendous uncertainty about his or her identity. That person then develops often a delusional system that becomes so fixed and so real in that person's mind that you can never shake it. One of the things that you learn if you ever work with mentally disturbed people, especially those who are quite paranoid is that the last thing in the world you ever want to do is argue with their delusional system. That is not helpful. Because the more that you argue with it, the tighter they are going to hold it, because that certainty that they hold within their minds is what keeps the terror of their uncertainty as a person from ever being experienced.

The more uncertain we feel about ourselves, the more certain we will have to pretend we are to the outer world. Someone who always has to be right and argues for the correctness of his or her position is waving a red flag that tells you, the extent of my saying I am right is the extent to which I believe I am wrong. That the more self-doubt I have, the greater will be my need to prove that I am always right and that everybody else is wrong.

Arguing with the Ego Proves the Ego Right

Q: In terms of what you are saying, whenever we argue with the ego, we would be making it stronger. It's a tricky thing then to be able to challenge the ego without arguing with it.

A: What you do with the ego is you simply smile at it. What the ego does with the ego is to argue with it and to fight with it. And obviously, if you argue with something, not only must you believe it's real, because otherwise, you wouldn't expend any effort in arguing with it; but what you are also saying is that you and I are different. That is the key idea. If I am arguing with you, I must believe you and I are different. And if you and I are different, my ego is home free. And of course, that is what a judgment is. I am judging that your belief system or your attitude or your this or your that is wrong and I am right. All that I am really doing is accentuating and proving that the ego is right.

What the Course would say, is that you can acknowledge differences with someone without making a big deal about it. So you believe A, I believe B. So what? We are both brothers or sisters in Christ. That is the reality and that is not different. There is no judgment on that. I can listen to what you say and I can say that doesn't make any sense to me. I don't believe that. If you do that in religious terms, someone can say that I believe God demands suffering and sacrifice. And I would say well, that doesn't ring true to me and that is not something that helps me. But it's perfectly okay if you believe that, and we can still be friends. And there is no judgment against you as a person. I can simply make a judgment without attack that says what you are believing doesn't help me, and obviously what I am believing doesn't help you. But what does that have to do with the fact that we are both one and the same?

The end of the ego system is the idea that we are all the same. The ego system thrives, because it began with that thought, that we are different. My survival as an ego depends on the fact that we are different. And it becomes extremely important that we be different. One of the ways I assert and affirm that we are different is that I am right. Again, you can always understand the extent of a person's self-doubt by the way that person will insist that he or she is right. It doesn't mean that you have to deny something you believe in. It is the insistence and the investment in being right, which automatically means you are proving somebody else wrong.

The only reason you would do that is because of the tremendous sense of self-doubt, inadequacy and uncertainty that you feel within. That is an example of the dynamic called reaction formation, where you feel something within that you deny, and you react and do the exact opposite. If I feel weak and awful inside, I'll act big and strong on the outside. A specific example of that would be what we call counterphobics. Those people, for example, who have phobias about heights and then, in order to prove that they are not afraid of heights will rent an apartment on the 20th floor of a building. What they are really doing is they are going to prove that they are not afraid of heights by doing something the exact opposite. All that they are really doing by fighting against their phobia is making it real.

That is a specific example of the more generalized dynamic of reaction formation. But that is what this passage is talking about. When I feel uncertain about myself, I must then defend against it by proving how certain I am. We are all so uncertain about our identity, because deep within our minds we know that we are not this separated self. The Course explains at one point, the ego is not aware of God, because it cannot be aware of something greater than itself. Yet it is aware there is something greater than itself. It doesn't know about God or about love, but it is aware that there is a part of our mind that can choose against the ego. That is what it's afraid of.

Meditation

As a start, I will begin by reading two short workbook lessons as a meditation. They are both found on page 456. They are Lessons 311 and 312, "I judge all things as I would have them be," and "I see all things as I would have them be." They are companion lessons which summarize basically all of the themes that we either have talked about already last night and we will talk about again today and tomorrow. These make the point, number one, that the ego first made judgment as a weapon against truth, as it says, as a way of proving that the unity and the love of Heaven is a lie and that separation and attack and guilt are what are true.

It does this because once we judge, then we see differences. And to see differences is to deny reality, which is always unity. We are the ones who made judgment, and we made judgment as a way of attacking and separating and killing. The Holy Spirit can yet use that same judgment as helping us to distinguish between the judgments of the ego and His own judgments—judgments of attack versus judgments of forgiveness. When that process of judging with the Holy Spirit is complete, that is what the real world is, which is mentioned here. At that point, we are able to accept God's loving judgment which always was. And that is that we are His beloved sons whom have never left Him and He's never left us.

All those ideas are found in these two lessons. So I'll read both of them and then we will spend a few moments in meditation.

(W-pII.311)
I judge all things as I would have them be.

Judgment was made to be a weapon used against the truth. It separates what it is being used against, and sets it off as if it were a thing apart. And then it makes of it what you would have it be. It judges what it cannot understand, because it cannot see totality and therefore judges falsely. Let us not use it today, but make a gift of it to Him Who has a different use for it. He will relieve us of the agony of all the judgments we have made against ourselves, and re-establish peace of mind by giving us God's Judgment of His Son.

Father, we wait with open mind today, to hear Your Judgment of the Son You love. We do not know him, and we cannot judge. And so we let Your Love decide what he whom You created as Your Son must be.

(W-pII.312)
I see all things as I would have them be.

Perception follows judgment. Having judged, we therefore see what we would look upon. For sight can merely serve to offer us what we would have. It is impossible to overlook what we would see, and fail to see what we have chosen to behold. How surely, therefore, must the real world come to greet the holy sight of anyone who takes the Holy Spirit's purpose as his goal for seeing. And he cannot fail to look upon what Christ would have him see, and share Christ's Love for what he looks upon.

I have no purpose for today except to look upon a liberated world, set free from all the judgments I have made. Father, this is Your Will for me today, and therefore it must be my goal as well.

"Projection Makes Perception"

There is a line in one of these lessons I would like to use as a springboard for what we will be talking about this morning, continuing actually what we did last night. The line that "Perception follows judgment" is very similar to the line which is repeated twice in the text, that projection makes perception (T-13.V.3:5;21.in.1:1). We first look within our

24

minds and perceive what we judge as reality there, and then we project that judgment onto the world and then perceive it there, as if it were really outside of us. In reality, of course, it's never left our minds, since as we discussed last night, ideas leave not their source.

We first look within our mind, which is where the ego is, and we make the judgment that we are different from God, that we have indeed separated from Him and that He indeed is now going to attack us for what we have done to Him. That is the original judgment. Differences are real, separation is real; and therefore, judgments against others are also real and justified. Once that judgment is made within our mind, we project it out and we therefore perceive a world of differences, a world of separation and a world of judgment. Obviously, also, a world of attack.

In reality, there is nothing outside of us. As we had discussed last night, there is nothing on the movie screen in front of us other than what has been projected from in back of us. Similarly, there is nothing that we perceive outside—all the differences we have made real—that have any existence or reality outside of the thought that originated in our mind. Since, again, ideas leave not their source, the idea of a separated world filled with differences, of good and evil, victim and victimizer, has never left its source which is in our mind, which once again means there is no world out there.

But the body was made, as we have seen, to tell us that there is indeed a world out there, so we spend all of our time invested in looking outside, rather than looking inside, which is not only where the original thought of judgment is and the thought of separation is, but where the loving judgment and the loving thought of the Holy Spirit is as well. If I don't look within but only look without, then I never can identify with the Holy Spirit's love, which means that my ego is home free. That is the basic modus operandi of the ego, to always have us look outside and judge what is outside rather than what is inside.

All things are echoes of the Voice for God (cont.)

Let's turn then to page 278 in the workbook, and pick up where we left off. We're on the second paragraph, and that of course, is the lesson "All things are echoes of the Voice for God."

(W-pI.151.2:1-3) You do not seem to doubt the world you see. You do not really question what is shown you through the body's eyes. Nor do you ask why you believe it, even though you learned a long while since your senses do deceive.

Clearly, this is true. None of us really doubts the reality of the world that we perceive. This is both true on the gross physical level, that we don't doubt that there is a world out there, there are people around us, that there is a lake outside, that the weather is rainy, etc., etc. None of us doubts that. And also, none of us doubts that the way we perceive this world is also true. None of us really doubts as we go through our day that our judgments about other people are wrong. We believe that everything that we think is true because we think it.

We never ask, which of course is the one question that the Course is really asking us to ask, "Why it is that we believe it?" And the answer for the reason why we believe that the world is real outside and that our judgments are real is because we don't want to look at the original judgment within us. Because the ego knows if we ever look at that original judgment that we have indeed separated from God, we would realize the whole thing is made up. And that is the ego's real fear.

As the Course explains, we believe our fear is of destruction and of crucifixion and of pain and suffering. But our real fear is of God's Love (T-13.III.1:11). Because that is what the ego is afraid of. In the presence of God's Love, just as in the presence of light, all darkness, all guilt, all fear, disappears. In the presence of the unity of that love, all belief in separation

26

disappears. That is the ego's fear, and that is why we believe what our body's senses tell us.

Again, our bodies were made specifically to keep hidden from us the truth that it's our mind that is perceiving. It is our mind that is thinking. And it's our mind that simply gives instructions to our body, to our sensory apparatus, to report back to us what it is we want to have reported back to us; namely, that there are differences and there are separations outside of us. Even more to the point, what our body's eyes bring back to us and our brain interprets for us, is that all the pain and the suffering that we experience is not our fault. Somebody else has done these things to us. We are the innocent victims.

The origin of that thought, of course, is that we are not responsible for the state of being outside of the kingdom. It is God Who has done it. That is why you find in the end of the Adam and Eve story in chapter 3 in the Book of Genesis, it is God Who ends up as the heavy. Because He's the one Who banishes Adam and Eve from the Garden. And He's the one who puts angels with a flaming sword to stand guard lest Adam and Eve would ever seek to return. And the message is very clear that because of our sin which God judges as a sin, not as a mistake, we are forever punished and banished from His Love. That is the underlying thought.

So it ends up, I am not responsible for being outside of the kingdom; God is. The horror of that thought is never allowed into awareness. Rather it becomes the reason I am unhappy right now in my daily life is because of what other people have done to me. My parents were not loving enough to me. They didn't give me enough, whether it was psychologically I didn't get enough, or materially I didn't get enough. My friends are untrue and unfaithful, my teachers aren't loving and trusting and accepting, my lovers or my spouses are not giving and loving enough and sensitive enough to my needs, my children are ungrateful, and on and on and on.

That's a fair statement, isn't it? (laughter) No one would disagree with that. But what we don't recognize of course is that seeing all that is coming from a belief, and it's a belief that comes from our need to have that be true. I want it to be true because that lets me off the hook, which specifically means it lets my mind off the hook, which even more specifically means that I am not in touch with that part of my mind that I call the decision maker. I am not in touch with that part of my mind that has *chosen* to feel victimized, and that has chosen to make my judgment real instead of God's Judgment.

(W-pI.151.2:4-5) That you believe them [believe our senses] **to the last detail which they report is even stranger, when you pause to recollect how frequently they have been faulty witnesses indeed! Why would you trust them so implicitly?**

This is true again, both on the gross level as well as on the more individual level. We all are aware of how our senses deceive us. We know that parallel lines do not meet, yet they appear to meet. If you are sailing on a boat, it certainly looks, as you gaze out to the horizon, that the sky meets the water. Everyone knows that that is not what happens, but that is what it looks like. There have been so many perceptual studies done on the phenomenon of closure, so that if people are shown a circle in which there is a slight break in it, people won't see the break and their eyes will automatically close the circle. Anybody who has ever done any proofreading knows how easy it is for the eye to skip over misprints or typographical errors. We are still finding typos in the Course, believe it or not, after God knows how many years.

Q: What would be the reason for our not wanting to see errors?

A: I think psychologically, the reason is that we don't want to perceive separation, because to perceive that there is a flaw in the printed word or in a circle or something, is to express

28

the fact that there is a flaw in me. And if there is a flaw in me, then that means it's because I have sinned against God and God is going to get me, and it brings back all of that. So that is the need to perceive wholeness. It is the ego's attempt to deny the lack of wholeness that we really know is true about ourselves. And then magically there is the hope that if I can perceive wholeness outside when it isn't there, then it means that I am whole, even though deep down I know that I am not whole, either.

Another perceptual illusion that everybody shares is that it certainly appears to all of us that the sun rises and sets, that the earth is stationary and that it's the sun that moves. We talk about the sun rising and the sun setting and those obviously provide many lovely experiences for people. But the truth of it is, as we also know, that it's the sun that is stationary and it's the earth that does all the movement. And it really is not the sun that rises and sets; it's the earth that rises and sets. However, it appears as if, to our eyes, as if it is the sun that rises and sets. We could multiply all these examples dozens and dozens of times, how our senses lie.

It is also the case that our psychological senses lie and how variable they are. We have all had experiences of being with people one day or one minute and we can't stand them, and then the next minute or the next day then we like them again. In fact, the phenomenon defies rational explanation every time. Things that we were so sure about once, we listen to or look at again, and they are different.

One year you may like one piece of music and hear it over and over again; the next year, you are bored stiff with it and something else excites you. Or a particular kind of painting or poetry or whatever. So that nothing is permanent. That is one of Jesus' ways of helping us understand why nothing in this world is real. Because God is permanent and God is unchanging, and God's Love is eternal. There is no shift, there is no change in Heaven.

In this world, everything shifts and changes. Bodies shift and change; thoughts shift and change; our minds shift and change; our attitudes shift and change. All of which form the proof that God could not have created any of this, because God's Love is unchanging and everything else here in the world is the opposite. That is what Jesus is talking about.

(W-pI.151:2:5-6) Why would you trust them [your senses] **so implicitly? Why but because of underlying doubt, which you would hide with show of certainty.**

We ended with this last night at the end of the first paragraph. The reason why it is so important that we be certain about what we perceive and what we think and what our judgments are is because that is our magical attempt to deny the uncertainty and the doubt that is underneath it. This is the same idea as what I was just responding to about why the law of closure works. We have the need to see wholeness outside of us because that is a way of denying the lack of wholeness we believe is real inside of us. Because I feel so filled with uncertainty and doubt about myself and my identity, it is imperative that I appear to be so certain and so confident and so sure of everything. And then if I can find dozens or hundreds or thousands of people who agree with me, then that is even better. Then my defense works even better.

As I mentioned last night, you can almost always tell the degree of uncertainty that a person feels by the degree of certainty that they attempt to project out. We are not talking about being right or being correct in one's judgments. We are talking about the *need* to be right and the *investment* in always being right. I always have to be right and you always have to be wrong. And we know very often that even when people are confronted with the objective fact that they have been wrong about something, there is still a part of them that has to deny it and says, "Yes, but. . . ." Or yes, I was wrong but I am really right if you look at it this way. If you turn it upside down, I am really right.

That is the same idea because if I am proven to be wrong about something that is external to me that is relatively inconsequential, that becomes the reminder that I was wrong right at the beginning in terms of God. If I was wrong about believing God is my enemy, and really God is my friend and God is my Creator and my Source, then it means that my ego was wrong. And to the extent that I identify with that ego, with that separated self, then to that extent, that means I will cease to exist. It is the ego's violent attempt to maintain its own self by attacking everyone and everything else. I must be right because if I am wrong, it means I no longer exist.

Now the Holy Spirit uses that as the argument for telling me, well, what is wrong with that—because the self you believe you are doesn't exist anyway. And if you can really say that you've been wrong, then you would realize that you have been right all along, because that thought of rightness has also been within you.

Another way of summarizing what the idea of the Course is, is that it's Jesus' way of saying to us, "Please listen to what I am telling you and you will recognize that what I am teaching you is truth, and what you've been teaching yourself is false. And you'll be much happier listening to what I tell you than what you've told you." There are two lines in the text, if you put them together, even though they come a few hundred pages apart, they say, "Resign now as your own teacher, for you have been badly taught" (T-12.V.8:3;28.I.7:1). And that is the point of the Course.

Jesus is trying to tell us you have taught yourself all these lessons and they have not made you very happy. Even aside from the fact that they are illusory and they are not true, they have not made you happy. Listen to what I am telling you and practice it, and you'll realize that not only is what I am saying true, but it will make you very happy. And that is how you'll find the peace of God.

Passages such as we find here in this lesson are designed to help us break down our identification with our body. And the brain is part of the body. It is not only breaking down our identification with the reality of what our body perceives, but also with what our body thinks. That is why there are two earlier workbook lessons (W-pI.10,45) which say that the thoughts you think you think are not your real thoughts. Well, if the thoughts I think I think, which are all the thoughts that I believe I am thinking, because I believe it's my brain that thinks—if all those thoughts are unreal, then what is real? It must be something that comes outside of my ego mind. The idea is first to recognize that we don't understand anything. And yet we are so sure that we are right all the time.

(W-pI.151.3:1-2) How can you judge? Your judgment rests upon the witness that your senses offer you.

This is a theme that is repeated many, many times. We will see it later on in the teacher's manual as well. *We cannot judge.* This is not talking on the level that I mentioned last night. In this world of the body, we must judge. Because that is what bodies do. It is talking on the metaphysical level that we cannot judge, because all of our judgments are based upon a thought that is not true. All of the judgments we believe are true in this world are done with the body, and are based upon again what our physical senses report to us, as well as what our past experience has taught us.

All of our judgments upon each other are based upon our past. We meet someone for the first time whom we don't know at all and we automatically make a judgment of that person. We don't like the way the person looks or the way the person dresses or the way the person talks or the way the person smiles or the way the person thinks. All of this is based upon the past. That is why one of the sections on special relationships is called "Shadows of the Past" (T-17.III). What we perceive in each other has nothing to do with the light of Christ that shines inside of each of us. It has to do with the shadows of the past that we carry with us in our mind and project onto each other.

(W-pI.151.3:3) Yet witness never falser was than this.

In other words, all of our judgments and our values are based upon what our senses tell us. But our senses lie. Remember, our senses lie because they were *made* to lie. Our computer was programmed to always tell falsity and to conceal truth—*always*. We know that this is true because our senses and our brain were specifically made to always get messages from outside of us. That is exactly what sensory organs do. They bring us back messages from outside of us.

Remember that messages that have to do with my own body are also outside of me, because the me is my mind. Whether my sensory apparatus brings me back messages that say my foot hurts or I have a stomachache or a headache, or it says that you are the pain in my neck and you have done something wrong, all of that information upon which I make a judgment is based on something that is external to me. That is why it's a lie. Because truth is inside of me. It is not outside of me. In fact, there is nothing outside of me. Everything that I perceive outside is really something that is a projection of what is within. All the judgments that we make are based upon that. That is why Jesus tells us that we can't judge.

(W-pI.151.3:4-7) But how else do you judge the world you see? [In other words, the world we see is judged by our sensory organs.] **You place pathetic faith in what your eyes and ears report. You think your fingers touch reality,** [In fact, I really believe that my fingers are touching the book that is here in front of me.] **and close upon the truth. This is awareness that you understand, and think more real than what is witnessed to by the eternal Voice for God Himself.**

We have made this outer world real, whether again it's the outer world that I perceive in bodies outside of me, or it's the outer world that I perceive within my own body. The perceptions and feelings and judgments upon my body are thoughts and experiences I have that I feel are within my mind which is really within my brain—all of these again come based upon perceptions of what appears to be outside of me. And there is nothing outside of me. The only true judgment we can make is to first identify with the Holy Spirit's love that is within our mind, and then we perceive outward. And everything that we see, as we will talk about later on in the workshop, is judged as either an expression of God's Love or a call for God's Love. That is the only judgment that the Course recognizes as being true in this world.

(W-pI.151.4:1-3) Can this be judgment? You have often been urged to refrain from judging, [Now what Jesus is talking about is, in the text, he says over and over again not to judge.] **not because it is a right to be withheld from you. You cannot judge.**

What he's telling us here is that we cannot judge because we don't understand anything. This is not talking about the Holy Spirit's judgment, and living in this world, we do have to make judgments. The idea again, as I mentioned last night, is that those judgments that we make should be done without guilt, without sin, without attack. That is what ensures that the judgments I make will not harm anyone, including myself.

Jesus is saying, "I am not telling you not to judge by taking something away from you. I am simply pointing out that you cannot judge." You *think* you can judge. Just as he's trying to help us recognize in the Course that we really cannot think, that the thoughts we think we think are not our real thoughts. The thoughts we think we think are defenses against our real thoughts. And ultimately, the thoughts we think we think are defenses against the real capital "T" Thought that we are—a Thought that is in the Mind of God.

The reflection of that Thought, with a capital "T," that we are in the Mind of God, is to be living in the real world, which is to identify with the Holy Spirit's love that is in our mind. But what this is helping us recognize, once again, is that all of our thoughts are specifically put there by our ego to conceal from us and defend against and attack the real thoughts that are there, which in this world, again, would be thoughts of forgiveness, thoughts of healing, thoughts of joining, thoughts of love. All of our thoughts of attack, all of our thoughts of separation, all of our thoughts of judgment, are specifically chosen to keep those underlying thoughts of love away from us.

We think we can judge, but in truth we can't. What *A Course in Miracles* is attempting to do is to substitute the thought system that Jesus is giving us for the thought system that the ego has given us. The ego's thought system again, which is judgment, attack, separation, death, is unreal; and therefore, are not really thoughts. The substitute for that, again, is the right-minded thought system of forgiveness and love, and those thoughts are the reflection of the thoughts that are true.

(W-pI.151.4:3-4) You cannot judge. You merely can believe the ego's judgments, all of which are false.

Early in the text, Jesus discusses how free will does not mean we can establish what our inheritance is as God's Son (T-in.1:4). It does mean that we are free to accept what that inheritance is or not. We are not free to put truth or take away truth in our mind. We are free rather to accept it or not. So we cannot judge, but we are free to believe that the ego's judgments are true. But that doesn't make them true. I can really believe there is a world out there, but that doesn't mean that there is a world out there. I can really believe you have done something terrible that has victimized me or other people whom I identify with, but that doesn't mean that you have actually done so. And we are not talking about behavior; we are talking about an attitude.

(W-pI.151.4:5) [The ego] It guides your senses carefully, to prove how weak you are; how helpless and afraid, how apprehensive of just punishment, how black with sin, how wretched in your guilt.

35

That basically covers the board, in terms of how we would think about ourselves. Everything we perceive and think and evaluate and judge is based upon the ego's need to have us believe what it just said. How helpless we are. How afraid, how black with sin and wretched in our guilt we all are. And our senses all do that. Now sometimes they do it in a direct way, where I judge myself against other people and always end up on the short end of the stick. And I believe that other people are smarter than I am and more handsome than I am and more beautiful than I am and more successful than I am, better *Course in Miracles* students than I am, more spiritually advanced than I am, etc.

Or it could be indirect, whereby I deny all those feelings about myself that I truly believe and I say the opposite. I say I am really much better than everybody else, I am much holier than everybody else, I am a much better *Course in Miracles* student than everybody else, on and on and on. Therefore I am justified in making all my negative judgments about other people. But either way, it's heads and tails of the same coin. Because I would not have the investment or the need to prove other people inadequate and inferior and wrong if I did not first believe that I was the one who was inadequate, inferior and wrong. Someone who truly knows who he is as God's Child doesn't have to prove it to anybody else.

But again, the purpose of the body is to prove how inadequate we are. And of course it ends up that way because the ultimate sense of inferiority is to see ourselves in relationship to God. That was the original judgment, if you remember. That God is the boss, God is the Creator, God is the authority and I am nothing. I am a measly little worm who is nothing and is just a dwarf next to this mammoth God Who thinks that He's the Source of all creation. The ego says, that's not fair; I am going to change it. I am going to steal all that power from God so I become great and God becomes little in comparison. That is again the original judgment that we all believe.

But deep within us, even though part of us tries to believe that we have stolen life and power and love from God, there is another part of us that knows that is not the case. And at some point, God is going to just get fed up with all this nonsense and come crashing through our defenses and destroy us. That is the underlying thought that everyone has. And that is what our body always tells us. Because our bodies are weak and inadequate and inferior and they die.

We have to take great care and spend tremendous amount of attention and effort and time to keep this body going, because it's always subject to breaking down. If it doesn't get fed on time, it starts to deteriorate. If it doesn't get enough sleep, and on and on and on. Our bodies are woefully inadequate to succeed in this world. And even when we think we have finally solved all the problems in the world and keep our bodies perfect, at some point, the body is going to die, which is the ultimate proof of how weak it is.

That is what the purpose of the body is. That is what the purpose of the world is. It is to give us the illusion of strength and of safety and of security and hope and love, but in reality, it ends up proving that we are nothing more than what we always knew. Just as it says here, we are helpless and afraid, apprehensive of punishment, black with sin, and wretched in our guilt. Our bodies reinforce that and yet attempt to put a cover over that thought, so that it appears as if we are just the opposite.

(W-pI.151.5:1) This thing it speaks of, [the "it" being the ego] **and would yet defend, it tells you is yourself.**

The ego tells us that our body is who we are. That is why people try to, again, do the opposite. That is the reaction formation we discussed last night. That the body really is a symbol of our wretchedness and our inadequacy and inferiority and nothingness, and yet we try to pretend that the body is a wonderful creation. Either it's a miracle of God's Love or it's a miracle of our own ingenuity or whatever, but the body is a wonderful apparatus. People extol the body and everything that the body can do for us. Or we extol the home of the body which is the world. That this is a wonderful world, it's a wonderful earth. In fact, it's a living earth; it's a living organism that has to be loved and taken care of, etc. Or there is a wonderful universe, cosmos. All attempts to deny what we really believe about ourselves, our bodies and the world.

Elsewhere, the Course describes the body as being a parody of God's creation (W-pI.95.2:1), or a cruel travesty of God's creation (T-24.VII.10:9). This is the ego's attempt to say to God, I can do you one better. And this wonderful body is the proof that I could do you one better. The horrifying truth, of course, is that we failed miserably.

Making Judgments in Our Classrooms

Q: You mention we're in this world, and we have to make judgments. In the practical sense of being in the world, my occupation is, I manage money. I have to make decisions on what's going to happen to the economy. Does "to judge or not to judge" have anything to do with those kinds of things?

A: Yes, it has to do with it. It doesn't mean you don't make judgments. It means you don't take the judgments that you make seriously. You look as if you take them seriously, and you do the best job that you can. If you are a parent, you be the best parent that you can be. If you are a money manager, you be the best money manager that you can be. If you are a student of *A Course in Miracles*, you be the best student you can be, because that is your classroom.

But at the same time that you are doing the best you can within the form of the classroom you've chosen, there is a part of your mind that realizes that it doesn't make any difference. What does make a difference is whether you do it with the love of God upholding you or with the guilt and the hatred of the ego upholding you. That is what makes a difference. It is the content and not the form. And the trick is to really be fully present to your world, to the people in your world, your responsibilities in your world and everything that is entailed in that, but at the same time, not letting it affect you.

What it means not "to take it seriously" is that you recognize that nothing that happens outside of you has the power to take away God's peace. No matter what the stock market does, even if you lose hundreds of thousand of dollars, or you make hundreds of thousands of dollars, the peace and the love of God is constant in you. And it's totally unaffected by what happens outside of you. That is what I mean by not taking it seriously.

The reason you chose the classroom of being a money manager, and the reason I chose the classroom that I am involved with and everybody has chosen his or her classroom is to learn that one lesson: that nothing outside of me can harm me, nothing outside of me can help me. The love and the peace of God that is within me is unaffected by anything else. That is the content that underlies everybody's classroom, everybody's lesson.

The form in which you have to learn it is different from the form in which I have to learn it and everyone else has to learn it. That is what you do. As you manage money, you do the best that you can. You make all the judgments that a money manager makes, or thinks he makes. But you realize that what you are really doing is learning that in the end, it doesn't matter because God's Love and God's peace is in everyone. It is in you, it's in your customers. That is the lesson. And we all have to learn it in different ways.

All things are echoes of the Voice for God (cont.)

I think we stopped on the fifth paragraph of that page. I read the first line. Let me read it again. We're back on page 278 in the workbook.

(W-pI.151.5:1) This thing it speaks of, and would yet defend, it tells you is yourself.

That is our body. The ego speaks of this body as being real, and we obviously believe that we are our bodies. And that is why we are so preoccupied with the pleasure and the happiness in the world being of this body, and the avoidance of anything that would cause us pain.

(W-pI.151.5:2) And you believe that this is so with stubborn certainty.

That is the same idea, that we are so sure we are right. We are so sure that this world is real. Just as centuries ago, people were so sure that the world was flat. People were so sure that the sun moved around the earth. We were so sure of that. People are so sure, even to this day, that human beings are the highest form of evolution. We are so sure, with a stubborn certainty, that our theology is correct, and everybody else's is wrong. People who study the Course are so sure that this is the only truth, and nothing else is true.

We are so sure about our judgments. And there is a stubbornness and there is an investment and a tenacity involved with it. That is what the Course is talking about. It is not saying that we shouldn't have preferences. We all have preferences and we all believe certain things. It is saying that we should become aware of the tenacious way with which we cling to the belief that we are right and other people are wrong. If I prefer a certain work of art to another, then I have to convince myself this is the greatest work of art that was ever made. The truth is that this is a work of art that pleases me and that I relate to, but it may not be the same for you. But what I have to do is prove that this is the greatest in the world because I say it is. That is what we do.

People who work with the Course and feel that it's God's personal gift to them; then feel that it must be God's personal gift to the whole world. If this is God's personal gift to the whole world, and I have made it my own, then it means that I am God's personal gift. Because that is the ego's way of aggrandizing itself.

(W-pI.151.5:3) Yet underneath remains the hidden doubt that what it shows you as reality with such conviction it does not believe.

Once again, anytime anyone stubbornly maintains something outside of themselves, it's a red flag that tells you they believe just the opposite about themselves. Because if I were truly happy and truly felt identified with God's Love, I would not have to maintain it with such a passion and such a stubbornness. If I were really so clear about a direction that my life was taking or what I was doing in my life, and I was really clear that this was what I was guided by love to do, I wouldn't have to convince anybody. I wouldn't have to be so stubborn about it. And I wouldn't have to feel that if things don't work out the way that I want them to work that something terrible is happening.

Whenever we have an investment in something external, whether it's something that has to do with another person, whether it has to do with health, whether it has to do with a particular preference, a thought system—whenever we have an investment in that, something that is external—it's always because we are so uncertain about who we are internally. I magically hope once again that if I can control what is outside of me and have what I want to be the case, then that will take care of what is inside of me.

If I did not have self-doubt, I would not have to be so damn cocky and so damn certain and positive about everything around me. Because I would realize that it doesn't matter what happens around me. All that matters is that the love of God is within me and I am that love of God. At that point, nothing external would matter. It made no difference to Jesus whether he lived or died on that last day of his life, because he knew he was not that body.

41

(W-pI.151.5:4) It is itself alone that it condemns.

That is what the ego condemns. In other words the fact that despite all of its furious attempts to be right and to be God, deep down in our mind is the thought that none of this has worked.

(W-pI.151.5:5-6) It is within itself it sees the guilt. It is its own despair it sees in you.

What this is talking about again is projection. Whatever it is that I attack in you and I feel despairing of outside is simply a mirror of what is inside of me. It is not your sin that I am attacking. It is not your sin that I am judging against; it's my own. It is not the hopelessness of the world outside of me, it's not the hopelessness of my own personal world outside that I am so involved with. It is the hopelessness that is within me, that I feel I've cast myself out of the kingdom and I'll never get back. That is why we all have such an investment in something outside of us.

Again, all judgment that we make external to us is nothing more than the reflection of the original judgment made inside of us. Except we forgot it. And that is the problem. And I believe that what I am perceiving out there is out there. Once I dump my negative judgments of myself onto you, I forget that I've done the dumping. I now believe that the negative judgments are outside of my mind, are firmly enshrined in you. And you are the one who is bad. It is the situation outside of me that is hopeless, not the situation within me that I've judged as hopeless.

Once again, what makes this course so simple is that everything is the same. We are not all the same only as Christ, and we are not the same only in terms of a classroom. Everything is the same in the sense that everything I perceive outside of me is always a reflection of what is inside of me. If I make something real outside of me by having a reaction to it, that is how I know it's real within me. In other words, the Course is not saying that everything that I perceive outside of me is within me. What it's talking about is if I have an investment in what I perceive outside of me, if I judge it as good or bad, if I judge it as minor or as major, if I judge it as good or as evil, then what I am doing is projecting that judgment from within me.

If I simply look outside and say, "Oh, that's what that person is doing," then there is not a projection. When Jesus was on the cross, he perceived people as driving nails into him. That was an objective fact within the dream. It was not an objective fact that people were attacking him, that people were vicious, that people were cruel, that God was ordering his sacrifice. That is not a fact; that was an interpretation. The fact was, people were just hammering nails. It is the interpretation that gives it all the meaning that it has for us.

It doesn't mean if you are watching somebody else hurt somebody else that that necessarily is what is going on inside of you. But if you find yourself upset about what you perceive outside and have a reaction to it, then you are making it real. And if you are making it real outside of you, it can only be because you first made it real inside of you. Otherwise, it would have no effect on you.

If I am judging something outside of me as having an effect on somebody else, whether it's me or anyone else, then I am making judgment real, I am making difference real, I am making separation real, which means I have first made that original judgment within myself real, that I have separated myself from God, I have established that there is in fact a difference between God and His Son, and that is now truth. The way that I know that I've made that truth is because I see it all around me. When the time comes, when you make no judgments between good and evil and between victim and victimizer, then you know that you've let go of all the judgments inside.

(W-pI.151.6:1-2) Hear not its voice. [The "its" of course is the ego.] The witnesses it sends to prove to you its evil is your own are false, and speak with certainty of what they do not know.

What is important about that first line, "Hear not its voice," is what is clearly implied in this is that there is a "you" that can choose whether to hear the ego's voice or not to hear the ego's voice. The "you" in this sense, is what we have been calling the decision maker. That is the part of our mind that chooses whether we will listen to the voice of the ego or the Voice of the Holy Spirit.

The importance of all this is that this represents our choice. The only sphere of activity in the entire universe rests within that part of our mind that chooses. Nothing happens anyplace else. If I am upset by something that appears to be happening to me here and I am judging it as having the power to hurt me or to please me or to hurt somebody that I identify with, and it appears as if there is something outside of me that is going on that has power to have an effect upon me, then in reality, all that is happening is that this part of my mind has chosen to give power to you or to the situation or circumstance I find myself in, and that's the issue.

Where the good news is in all of that is if I am the one who has chosen to experience myself as capable of being hurt by you, and that is what judgment ultimately is all about, then therefore, I am the one who can change that. I can't change you, and as we all know. It is extremely frustrating to attempt to try to change things in the world and to get them to work out in such a way that will please us and make us happy. Because the world has a terrible way of not cooperating. Sometimes it seems to; other times, it doesn't. Which means that our fate and our happiness and our hope is always dependent upon the whims of other people or the whims of the weather or the whims of God or the whims of whatever it is that is judged to be outside of us. But to recognize that everything that occurs and everything that I experience as occurring is coming from within my own mind, gives me all the power.

As the Course explains at one point, we are in control of the universe, not Heaven, not the Universe of God. But we are in control of this universe in terms of how we experience it. Since ultimately, there is nothing outside of our minds anyway, then there is nothing to control outside. But there is something to control or to choose between in our own mind. And that is where our power rests.

That basically is the whole meaning of judgment. That is why, again, Jesus says that we cannot judge. Because it's the ego in us that cannot judge what it doesn't understand. But the one judgment that we can make and that the purpose of the Course is to train us to make, is the judgment between the ego's voice and the Holy Spirit's Voice. When Jesus says here, hear not the ego's voice, what he's telling us is that we have another choice.

One of the most effective things the ego did right at the beginning was not only to drown out the Holy Spirit's Voice, but to drown out the memory of his Voice, which means that we no longer even think that there is another way of looking. Just as, on another level, we never even think about that there is another way of looking at this physical world, which again is what the quantum physicists are helping us to recognize. All matter is simply just a form of thought or just an expression of thought. The world is not what we think it is. But we have never stopped to think, well maybe there is another way of looking at the physical universe; maybe there is another way of looking at the psychological universe.

What the Course is trying to help us realize is that there is another Voice. There are two thought systems in our mind and we can make a choice. Up until this point, we never knew we had a choice. Our only choices lay within the ego system. I could choose one illusion which would be less painful to me than another illusion. But I never knew I had the choice to dismiss all the illusions as one, and choose the one Voice and the one thought that would lead me beyond everything in this world. That is what the purpose of this world is—to help us realize, again, that we are not the ones who can make judgments. So that second line, which I'll reread.

(W-pI.151.6:2) The witnesses it [the ego] sends to prove to you its evil is your own are false, and speak with certainty of what they do not know.

There is a section in "The Obstacles to Peace" called "The attraction of guilt," which explains this dynamic very, very powerfully (T-19.IV.*i*). It talks about how we send out two messengers—either a messenger of fear or a messenger of love. And those messengers bring back to us those messages which we have decided first we want. I first make a judgment that I want to see evil and sin all around me so I don't have to see it within myself. And then I send out a messenger that will seek out proof that this world is indeed a hostile, terrible place and that I am vulnerable and the innocent victim of what other people do to me. I first have made a decision that's what I want to experience. I then give that instruction to my brain, which then will look out into this world and will seize upon anything it can find that will prove to me that what I am believing is true.

Now the problem is not the message that is brought back to me. The problem is the messenger I sent out. I first made a decision to see myself as guilty and then blame everybody else for it. I then seek justification for that in everything and everyone around me. The problem is not what I perceive outside; the problem is what I first judged against within myself. I judged against myself, which is within my mind. I then no longer assume responsibility for it, and I say the reason I am so unhappy is because of what somebody else has done to me. And that is what it means here when it says the ego's witnesses are false, and they "speak with certainty of what they do not know." They don't know what truth is. They don't know what true judgment is. They think that they know.

I become convinced that you have treated me unfairly. And I have forgotten that I first made a decision to believe that I've been treated unfairly and then I want to find a corroboration for it. And then I use you as a scapegoat for that. I could just as easily, as it says later on in that section, choose a messenger of love. And then I see what you have done, which may be exactly the same thing that my ego is seeing, but the interpretation is different. Rather than seeing you as someone who is evil and sinful and hurting me or others, I see you as my brother or sister in Christ who is calling out for the same love of God that you believe is denied to you. And it's the same love that I believe is denied me.

(W-pI.151.6:3) Your faith in them [our faith in the ego's witnesses] **is blind because you would not share the doubts their lord can not completely vanquish.**

In this world, we use the expression "blind faith." We have faith in something that we really can't see. So we put faith in the ego's witnesses, even though we can't see them. We can't understand them because they are not there. In other words, what the ego tells us is all made up. The ego of course is the lord, and the doubts that they cannot completely vanquish is the nagging doubt that ultimately I am wrong and God is right.

(W-pI.151.6:4) You believe to doubt his vassals is to doubt yourself.

The ego's vassals would be its witnesses; in other words, basically, the body, and all the things that the body tells us. And of course, the fear in all this is that if I really learn to doubt what my body tells me is true and the world tells me is true, since I am identified with that body and the world, then I will no longer be true. That is the fear.

That is another way of understanding one of the major themes of the Course. It is trying to help us shift our identification from the ego to the Holy Spirit. The ego's identification is very much rooted in the body, but the body is seen as separate and the body is seen as vulnerable and as weak and as guilt-ridden and as sinful. And that is the self that we all identify with.

The Course tries to help us shift that identity to a Self that is holy and that is sinless and that is guiltless. We are not asked to deny that we are in a body. We are asked to deny the ego's interpretation of being in a body. When the Course tells us not to see our brothers as a body, it does not mean to deny the physical experience of a body sitting opposite us. What it's telling us to do is to deny the ego's purpose for the body. My ego's purpose for your body is to see you as someone who is separate and different. Either someone whom I could steal from under the guise of love, which is what special love is, or I steal from under the guise of hate, which is when I just kill you. But that is the purpose that bodies serve in the ego's system, that meet our needs.

Again, Jesus is not asking us to deny our bodies or other people's bodies. He's simply asking us to shift the purpose, so that now the purpose that your body serves from his point of view is that you become a classroom in which I learn what forgiveness is. A mistake many people make with the Course, is that they think we are being asked to deny the body or that the body is seen as evil or sinful or bad. It doesn't say that.

In fact, there is a wonderful passage in the workbook where Jesus says, "And this above all I need. That you will hear my voice and give it to the world. I need your voice, your hands, your feet, through which I save the world" (W-rV.in.9:2). He's very clearly telling us that the body, given over to him, becomes holy. The body is not holy in and of itself, but holy because it serves his purpose. Just as he used Helen's body as a vehicle for bringing his words of love into the world, so he uses everyone else's body, which means that the judgment that we now make upon the body is not that it's evil or sinful or separating, but rather is a judgment of love because it serves the purpose of love.

But as long as we believe that we are this body and it serves the ego's purpose of attack and separation and judgment, then we believe to give up attack, separation and judgment means we will be without ourselves and we will cease to exist. That is why we cling so insanely and yet stubbornly to holding onto the judgments that we make and to believing that we are right and God is wrong; or we are right and another person is wrong. We don't want to be proven wrong. We know what is right.

We not only know what is right for ourselves, but we believe we know what is right for other people as well. That is the height of the ego's arrogance. The only way we can begin the process of doubting the ego's thought system is to begin to question some of its premises. And the premises that we can begin to question without having to dismiss the whole thought system, are the premises that I can really be affected by what other people do. That is a pretty shabby judgment on ourselves to believe that my peace is so flimsy and so weak that the slightest thing that somebody else does can take it away from me.

We know, for example, in our special love relationships, that if the loved person somehow doesn't look at us quite right and doesn't quite act as exuberant and as loving as the person did yesterday, our whole world is shattered. And we all know how painful that can feel. But if we can step back and say, isn't this absurd—just because a person looks a little funny at me, I believe the whole love and peace of God in me has been taken. Not only is that a shabby image of ourselves, but it's a shabby image of God's Love. It is so weak and unstable that a slight shift in tone of voice, or because a person calls two minutes later than he or she said he or she would call, that that has the power to totally change and turn into upheaval the love and peace of my own mind. But that is what we believe.

What salvation then becomes is to begin the process of simply looking at that. When I find myself devastated because you haven't done the simple little thing that you used to do, that became such a symbol of love for me, and I find myself shattered by that—if I can simply step back and say oh, I am shattered by this. I must have identified with this ego self again. Because I am afraid of the true majesty and the true magnitude of God's Love. Again, all we have to do is look at it. Just observe what our egos do and how absolutely silly they are, and the tremendous power we give to something that is outside of us, which means the attack that we really make is upon the power of our own mind.

(W-pI.151.7:1) Yet you must learn to doubt their evidence will clear the way to recognize yourself, and let the Voice for God alone be Judge of what is worthy of your own belief.

What we do have to learn, which again is the purpose of the Course, is that to doubt the body's evidence, or the evidence that the body brings to us is the way that we will remember who we are. Rather than ourselves ceasing to exist by doubting the reality of the body's judgments, what will happen is that we will remember who is truly existing in us. We really have to recognize that the way to find peace is to give up judgment. The way to find peace is to begin the process of doubting the validity of what we have made so real for ourselves.

Again, one of the key ways of understanding how that works is to recognize how much we place our self-worth and our happiness on what other people do or what the world does. If I make plans to have a picnic on a day, for example, and then it rains and the picnic is canceled and I feel disappointed and I feel upset, what I am doing is saying that the weather really has power over God's Love. Because I could be just as peaceful and feel just as much love today whether the sun shines or it rains; it doesn't matter.

That doesn't mean I don't have a preference. But if the preference doesn't work out, it doesn't mean that my whole world has shattered. That is what is important. And that is the judgment again that we continually make, that we are weak and impotent and inadequate and shabby and that the outer world has power to make us happy and feel better. And again, the idea behind the statement that we should let the Voice for God be the judge of what is worthy of our own belief is clearly implying that we have first made the wrong choice and let the ego be the judge. But we can make another choice.

(W-pI.151.7:2) He will not tell you [meaning the Holy Spirit] **that your brother should be judged by what your eyes behold in him, nor what his body's mouth says to your ears, nor what your fingers' touch reports of him.**

In other words, the Holy Spirit's presence of love in our mind doesn't base its judgments on what happens physically. It doesn't base its judgments on what people do or what they say. It doesn't base its judgments on what the ego tells us these people are. The Holy Spirit's judgment is not something that is perceptual. It is not bound or conditioned by anything of this world. The Holy Spirit's judgment obviously is that we are all children of the same God and we all share the same light and the same love.

(W-pI.151.7:3) He passes by such idle witnesses, which merely bear false witness to God's Son.

In other words, the Holy Spirit doesn't look to the body, doesn't let His judgment rest upon what happens outside. By asking His judgment to become our own, what He's asking us to do is also not to let our judgment and our experience of love and peace, whether it's experience about ourselves or toward someone else, be conditioned by or dependent upon what other people do. Because this is the way that we all live in this world. I will love you and feel good about you if you behave a certain way or act a certain way or speak a certain way or live a certain way or think a certain way. And if you depart from that, then my love will change.

The reason, of course, that we all act like that towards each other, is because that is the way we believe God acts towards us, which is because we believe that is how we acted towards God. We believed that God loved us as long as we were good little boys and girls and stayed home with Him. The moment that we grew up and separated from Him, we believed He was angry. And so we believe that God's Love changed; that God changed His Mind about us.

Again, we believe that God changed His Mind about us because we accuse ourselves of changing our minds about Him. One moment we are happy being with God in Heaven and the next moment saying to God, what you have given me is not enough. I want something more than Everything. I want something more than Perfect Love. I want something more than eternity and something more than infinity. I want separation and I want hate and I want misery and I want pain and I want death. Except the ego doesn't tell us that is what we said.

But it was our love that changed, which we then made real in our minds by judging against it, taking it seriously, remembering not to laugh at it. We then projected it out and said we didn't change; God changed. God now has become vindictive and vengeful and angry and inconsistent in His love. That became such a terrifying thought that we denied the whole mess. But then the mess still remained real.

The thought of separation remained real in our mind, we projected it out into the world, and we now saw outside on the screen that same scenario and that same script that we made real inside; namely, that love is not constant, love changes, love is conditional. Love has to be earned, love has to be bought, love has to be bargained for, love has to be traded for; and especially, love can hurt us. That is what the purpose of the body is. The ego made up the world and the body to be the false witness that witnesses to the seeming truth of all this.

(W-pI.151.7:3-4) He passes by such idle witnesses, which merely bear false witness to God's Son. He [meaning the Holy Spirit] **recognizes only what God loves, and in the holy light of what He sees do all the ego's dreams of what you are vanish before the splendor He beholds.**

What God loves is the Christ in us, and there is nothing else. That is all the Holy Spirit sees. He doesn't see the illusions because there are no illusions. If He saw the illusions and acted against the illusions we have made real, then again, He would be as insane as we are. His love and His light then shines as the living presence within our minds of what is true.

One of the key themes in the Course is that we are not to bring truth to illusions, but bring illusions to truth. To believe the Holy Spirit operates in the world and corrects the illusions of the world is to bring the truth to the illusion. In other words, we make up this miserable world, make it absolutely hopeless and then say to God, "Now that I've made this, please come here and fix it for me." And that is bringing truth to the illusion.

I made up a belief in scarcity that is now manifesting itself as scarcity in terms of not having a parking space, or not having good physical health or not having enough money. All of that is a product of my belief in scarcity, which I now say is not my belief in scarcity; it's something that is tangible. I don't have a parking space. I can see that. I don't have good physical health; I can see that. The size of my bank account is dreadfully low; I can see that. And that is real.

I now drag God down from His throne in Heaven and say, "Here, Big Guy, fix this for me." Even though I made this up to attack Him, I now say, "Here, fix it for me because that is what a loving God is supposed to do." That is bringing truth to the illusion. That is why deep down, we all hate God because He doesn't play the game with us. Because what God says, through His memory in our mind, is don't ask Me to come to what doesn't exist to fix it. Rather, you come back to the place that you wandered away from. That is what the illusion is.

The problem is not the scarcity of the parking space, or the scarcity of money or the scarcity of this or that. The problem is the thought of scarcity, which is the thought that you've been separated from that light and that love in your mind. Come back to that light and love and I hold it open for you. That is what Jesus says at one point: I stand at the door and I hold the door open for you. I can't take you through it, but I stand at the door. Light and that love stands at the door and calls you back. That is what bringing the illusion to the truth is.

We wandered off into the world of illusion. We wandered away from truth. Now we wander back to the world of truth, which is in our mind. That is what God recognizes. That is what the Holy Spirit recognizes. Once we are back in that presence of love in our mind, which is the real world and never leave it again, then all the ego dreams vanish. It doesn't necessarily mean that the world will vanish in that instant, but what it does mean is that all my dreams of sin and of pain and of suffering and of death—that is what vanishes. The thoughts will vanish.

(W-pI.151.8:1-2) Let Him be Judge of what you are, [and obviously implied here, instead of the ego] **for He has certainty in which there is no doubt, because it rests on Certainty so great that doubt is meaningless before Its face. Christ cannot doubt Himself.**

It takes a separated mind to doubt itself. It takes a dualistic consciousness that can step back and look at itself and form a judgment and an opinion about that self. Christ in Heaven, as I mentioned last night, doesn't have a split awareness, doesn't have a dualistic mind. Christ cannot look at Himself in relationship to God, because to do so involves a split consciousness. There is no split in Heaven. It is perfectly unified.

(W-pI.151.8:3-4) The Voice for God can only honor Him, rejoicing in His perfect, everlasting sinlessness.

Whom He has judged can only laugh at guilt, unwilling now to play with toys of sin; unheeding of the body's witnesses before the rapture of Christ's holy face.

The idea of laughing at guilt I'm going to leave for now. We will come back to it at the end of the lesson. But I do want to comment briefly on this idea about "unwilling now to play with toys of sin." I mentioned earlier that often in the Course Jesus talks to us as if we were little children. We are little children in the sense of not understanding. One of the ways the Course helps us recognize how silly this whole world is, is to speak about sin, which of course is the most egregious thing in the whole world—everything here is sin.

The course talks about what we judge as being sin as simply being little childish toys. It talks about toys of sin. To us, sin is not a toy. To talk about the holocaust where thirteen million people were killed, as a toy, is not what the world experiences. To talk about someone who brutally rapes and kills dozens of women, to say that is simply just a toy, that is just a silly child's game—that is not what our experience is.

Our experience is just the opposite. In reality, these are just toys because they come from a silly thought that had no effect at all. Sin seems so real to us and so awful, whether I talk about a personal sense of sinfulness or awful in the sense of the sin that I perceive around me. Sin seems so awful and grandiose and powerful only because we believe it had the power to destroy God. That is where the power of sin in our world comes from.

We believe the tiny, mad idea, that one judgment that we made against ourselves and against God was powerful enough that it could destroy Heaven, and that it could rupture the unity of God's Love. That God's Son can now sever himself from his Father and declare himself on his own. That is what sin is all about. That is the power that we have given to sin.

The truth of it is that absolutely nothing has happened. In a symbol of Heaven's song, the song of Heaven, the Course talks about that "not one note in Heaven's song was missed" (T-26.V.5:4) because of that "tiny, mad idea" (T-27.VIII.6:2). Heaven never even knew that anything happened, for the simple reason being that nothing happened. But we thought that the tiny, mad idea (that we could be separate from God) occurred and was such an awful thing that happened, that we had to make up an entire world to defend against that thought.

The awfulness of that thought of sin, the awfulness of that judgment, then gets projected from our mind into this world. This world is literally the thought of sin or the thought of guilt crystallized. That is what the world is. It has no reality and no substance other than that which guilt gives it. You take away the thought of guilt and the world disappears, which means this world has no power at all. Because sin has no power.

That is why, again, the Course talks about toys of sin (W-pI.151.8:4;153.13:3;W-pII.4.5). That is what Jesus means when he says we learn how to laugh at guilt. That is what he means a little later on in the workbook when he says that we learn to laugh at pain, at sickness, starvation, poverty and death. He doesn't mean laugh at it in a derisive way or insensitive way or unfeeling way. He means laughing at it because it has no power over the love and the peace of God that is within us.

To be upset by anything in the world is really to say sin has power. Because if I really stood in my mind with the presence of God's Love—if I really knew Jesus was with me, and his love and his peace was all that I was, and am and will ever be—nothing in this world would have any power over me. Which means anything that I believe has power over me, power to hurt me or anybody else, is coming from the belief that I am separate from that presence of love in my mind. Which means the problem is not what goes on in the screen outside; the problem is the film I am running through the projector in my own mind.

That is what I meant earlier when I said the only sphere of activity that occurs in this whole universe is within that part of our mind that chooses. That is why there is such a strong emphasis in the Course on choosing and deciding, over and over and over again. The very end of the text has the section, "Choose Once Again." It is the power to choose which is the power of the universe. There is no other power here. It is not the power that your body has over me. It is not the power that my body has over me. It is the power that my mind has, that it can really believe that the illusion is reality, and that the dream is reality.

In truth, it is only silly toys that children play with. If you watch a little child play and the child is playing soldiers or playing house or whatever, the child really gets totally engrossed and identified with what he or she is doing. And will get angry, get sad, get exhilarated, get disappointed—as if there were real people in front of him. In reality, as an adult, we look at it and realize it is simply a toy, it is simply a game and has no reality and no effect on the reality of that child. Just as, if you want to comfort a child who's just had a terrifying nightmare, one of the things you'll do is say to the child, "It was all a bad dream and you are still here with mommy and daddy. Nothing has changed. It was all a bad dream."

Well, that is what the whole Course is about. Jesus is having us look at everything in this world which seems to be so monumental and so powerful and awesome in what it can do, and simply says to us, "Isn't this silly? It is just a silly dream in which nothing has happened. You are just playing with toys. You think you are playing with cannons and with rifles and with bombs in which real people can be hurt." And he's telling us, "It's nothing; it's all make-believe."

If you take a small child, to a puppet show and the child becomes upset because one of the puppets that he identifies with dies, one of the things that you would do to comfort the child is explain that it was all make-believe, that it was simply a lifeless piece of wood that fell over. No one was hurt. The child doesn't understand that because the child believes that what he perceives is real, even though you as the adult understand that it's all make-believe.

That is exactly the position that Jesus is in with us. He's an older brother, who's taken all of us little, little children to a puppet show. We sit in the puppet show which is our life and we look at what goes on and we become what goes on. I become what happens to this body. I become what happens to your body, and what happens to your body has an effect on me. What happens to my body has an effect on me. I get really upset or I get really happy if it works out the way that I want.

Sitting next to me is my loving older brother who says, "There, there, don't be upset. Nothing is happening. It is all make-believe. These are only toys of sin that you are perceiving. It is not anything real. It seems to be outside of you, it seems to be something that is real, but it's all something that is make-believe." That is why he talks about toys of sin.

There is a wonderful workbook page that answers the question, "What is sin?" And at the end of it he says, "shall we not put away these sharp-edged children's toys?" (W-pII.4.5:2). They appear to be sharp edged because they hurt us. As we know bodies can hurt. There is a line in the text that says, "Are thoughts dangerous?" And the answer is, "To bodies, yes!" That is as long as I identify with my body. If I do, these children's toys of sin can have very sharp edges and they can cut and they can hurt. But when I realize that they are only toys and that they have no effect on me or anybody else, then I realize the whole thing is make-believe and I've taken a major step towards awakening from the dream. That is the judgment that we are asked to make.

The "Hero" of the Dream

Turn in the text to page 587. This section, of which I am only going to read a part, I think is one of the most powerful ones in the Course in explaining, number one, how and why the Holy Spirit doesn't do anything in the world. It explains what this world really is, what the connection is between the world and the mind, and ultimately, of course, how one undoes all the pain and the suffering that we experience here.

I am going to start reading from page 587 but before I do that, I am going to just comment briefly on the third paragraph on page 586. The title of this section is called "The "Hero" of the Dream." The hero is the body. The previous section is called "The Dreamer of the Dream," and both of these sections really form a unit. The point of all of this is, is to have us recognize that we are the dreamer. Our mind is the dreamer and our world outside is the dream. The dreamer is the cause of what is perceived outside as the dream, not the other way around.

The ego would have us believe the dream is dreaming us. That the dream, the world, the bodies outside, which again include my own body, is the cause. The effect is that I am feeling upset, I am feeling sad, I am feeling happy. My well-being, my sense of peace, my sense of love, is dependent upon what the world does or does not do for me. The dream is dreaming me. The point of these two sections is to have us recognize that we are the dreamer of the world of dreams that is outside of us. I cannot change the dream, but I can change the mind of the dreamer, which is me. The Course says earlier, "Therefore, seek not to change the world, but choose to change your mind about the world" (T-21.in.1:7).

(T-27.VIII.6:1) Let us return the dream he gave away unto the dreamer, [in other words, that we have perceived the dream as separate from us, and now let's return the problem back to the mind where it is] **who perceives the dream as separate from himself and done to him.**

That is the idea that the dreamer is the innocent victim of what the dream has done to him. In reality, it's the other way around. That it is the dreamer that has "victimized" or has caused what the dream is.

(T-27.VIII.6:2) Into eternity, where all is one, there crept a tiny, mad idea, at which the Son of God remembered not to laugh.

That is what we have already been talking about. In the instant that that one judgment seemed to arise, that one perception of differences seemed to arise, the problem was we took it seriously instead of looking at it and laughing, and saying isn't it silly, isn't it absurd, isn't it preposterous, that a part of God could actually separate from Him and declare itself as God. The thing is just silly. What we did in fact is say this is very serious, this is awful, and I must now defend myself against that thought of guilt and the terrifying thought that God is going to punish me. That is what it is going to talk about.

(T-27.VIII.6:3) In his forgetting [In other words, in the Son of God's forgetting to take this as a joke, forgetting to laugh] **did the thought become a serious idea, and possible of both accomplishment and real effects.**

The accomplishment is what we call sin. I actually have accomplished this tiny, mad idea of being separate. The effects of the thought of sin is the world that is perceived outside of us. And then Jesus says:

(T-27.VIII.6:4) Together, we can laugh them both away....

Meaning joining with him, because remember, he's the manifestation of the Holy Spirit. In that original instant, we chose to separate from the Holy Spirit's laughter, which was simply saying, "Isn't this silly?" We chose to separate from that, making it serious. Then within the dream, within the world of form, Jesus—certainly for us in the western world— became the one who manifested the Holy Spirit's Atonement principle. He says to us from the cross, isn't this silly to believe that the love of God can be affected by a silly nail that is driven into a body that is not even there. Nothing is happening. When he asks us to join with him, it is the same thing as asking us to join with the Holy Spirit. He's asking us to join with that presence and that thought of love in our mind that has us look at everything in this world and smile at it, which we will see on the next page. So he says again:

(T-27.VIII.6:4-5) Together, we can laugh them both away, [and what the both is, is the thought of sin that has been accomplished and the thought of sin that is made manifest in the world—the so-called real effects] **and understand that time cannot intrude upon eternity. It is a joke to think that time can come to circumvent eternity, which *means* there is no time.**

It is simply a joke to believe that the tiny, mad idea has any power over God. In an image that Jesus uses earlier that he borrowed from Peter Sellers, he talks about the ego's being a tiny mouse that roars at the universe (T-21.VII.3:11). That is all the ego is. It is not a raging lion that is roaring, which is an image that you find in Peter's second letter in the New Testament, where he talks about the devil that way. The ego is not this raging lion. It is a frightened little mouse that roars at the universe. And if you just try to hold a picture of that, then you realize how ludicrous everything is.

Now turn to page 587, the second paragraph. I'll start reading from the middle of that second paragraph.

(T-27.VIII.8:4) It is not easy to perceive the jest when all around you do your eyes behold its heavy consequences, but without their trifling cause.

What is important about this is Jesus recognizing that within this world, within the illusion, it is extremely difficult to look at all the heavy consequences of sin, all the things that go on, and realize that they are simply silly. Because it is true, when you cut off the effect from the cause and you only look at the effect, which is this world, then there is no question, terrible things happen here. It is only when you put the effect, the world, in its proper perspective and context as being simply the consequence of the tiny, mad idea of being separate from God; at that point, everything then becomes silly.

But when you believe you are a body and you believe that you are surrounded by bodies, then when a body dies or is brutally raped or killed or burned or gassed, then that is something that is not silly. That becomes very real and becomes very tragic. Within the illusion, within the world of effects, separated from the cause in the mind, the world does seem very real and very painful. Again it is not easy to perceive the jest, to see how silly all of this is, when all that you see is only what is outside of you.

And of course, then we make a judgment. This is why we are told over and over again that we cannot judge. I judge what goes on outside of me and I say this is good and this is bad. I say here's a certain person who's a real evil person or a criminal and vicious and sinful, and here's someone who's a saint. I judge what is outside as if there was something outside of me, and as if there are things outside of me that are different one from the other. And that is only because I have forgotten that what I am perceiving outside is coming from what I first perceived and made real within me. When I go back within my mind and I look at what is inside and I say, yes, the reason I see everything is so terrible outside is because I first made everything terrible inside, but there is nothing terrible inside. Then I go back outside and I look and I smile.

(T-27.VIII.8:5) Without the cause do its effects seem serious and sad indeed.

When you split the cause from the effect, then the effects do seem serious and sad and with very, very heavy consequences. But when you join up the effect with the cause, then you realize that cause itself is trifling. That is the tiny, mad idea. Sin only seems to be a roaring lion. Sin only seems to be a solid wall of granite that we cannot get through (T-22.III.5:6). It is only when we really look at what sin is, we realize it is a silly little mouse that believes it can destroy the universe, or that it is just a tiny wisp of black smoke or a little series of feathers that just blow aimlessly in the wind (T-18.I.7:6). It is not a solid wall of granite.

But if I don't look at it and I take what the ego has told me as truth, then I feel sin is this raging lion and is this solid wall of granite, and it will never change. It will never change within me and it will never change without me in terms of you. But when I do look at it, which is why it is so important to simply be able to look at the ego, I realize it is no big deal. What I judged to be so terrible outside, when I put it in its proper perspective as this simple effect of the cause, and the cause is silly, then the effect must be silly, too. That is how I learn how to laugh at it.

(T-27.VIII.8:6-7) Yet they but follow. [The effects but follow the cause.] **And it is their cause that follows nothing and is but a jest.**

The cause follows nothing because sin doesn't exist. The belief in our sinfulness, the belief in guilt, is the cause of this world. But sin itself has no cause because it doesn't exist. We have never separated from God. That is what the Atonement principle is. We have never separated from God. And therefore, sin itself, if it has no cause, is not an effect. It doesn't exist. And therefore, obviously it can't cause anything else. The whole thing is made up. As they say, it is all done with smoke and mirrors. That is what the ego has done with the world. The whole thing is done with smoke and mirrors. There is nothing here. It just looks as if there is something here.

(T-27.VIII.9:1) In gentle laughter does the Holy Spirit perceive the cause, and looks not to effects.

This is a very, very important line and this is one of the really helpful ways of understanding why the Holy Spirit doesn't do anything in the world. What the Holy Spirit judges is not the effect. He doesn't judge anything in the world as needing help. He doesn't judge anything in the world as needing healing. He doesn't judge anything in the world as needing anything because there is nothing in the world.

What He judges is the cause, which is the belief in sin or the belief in separation. And His judgment of the cause is, isn't that silly, that a part of God could be separate from its Source. That is the judgment. Once you believe the Holy Spirit does things for you in the world, He is making the error real, as this says in the next line.

(T-27.VIII.9:2) How else could He correct your error, who have overlooked the cause entirely?

How could he help us if he also overlooks the cause, as we have done? The problem, the reason I am so upset in the world, is because I have forgotten where the world came from. I have only looked to the effects. That is the purpose of my body, only to make the effect real, and to totally split off and deny the existence of the cause, which is my belief in my mind. I've overlooked this cause entirely. I've only looked to the effect. I make the effect real. There is no way that I can help myself. There is no way that I can judge anything outside of me, because I have forgotten about where it came from. There is no way I can understand how anything in this world works, because I have forgotten what makes this world work, which is guilt in my mind.

That is why Jesus tells us over and over again that we don't know anything, we can't understand anything, we can't judge anything. Because we have split everything off and we have forgotten that everything outside is simply the reflection of what is inside. We have forgotten the cause. The purpose of the Holy Spirit, His function, is to remind us of the cause. That is the purpose of the miracle. That is why this is called *A Course in Miracles.*

It is not called *A Course in Love.* It is not called *A Course in Finding Parking Spaces.* It is called *A Course in Miracles.*

What the miracle does, as explained in the next chapter, is that the miracle restores to cause the function of causation (T-28.II.9:3). What that translates to is that the miracle restores to the mind, which is the cause, its function of being the causative agent. What the miracle does is bring our attention away from the world that is perceived outside of us back within us, and says the cause of the suffering in the world, the cause of my suffering, is my mind.

That is what the miracle does. It brings the problem back from outside to within. It brings the illusion back to the truth. What magic is, which is the Course's way of understanding how the ego functions, which is the exact opposite of the miracle, is bring the truth to the illusion. Most people's experiences of God and of the Holy Spirit is of a magical figure, who will come into the illusion and fix it. That is why it is a gross distortion of what the Course is teaching to believe the Holy Spirit does something for you in the world.

Jesus talks to us often like that in the Course because that is the only way we can understand it. But we will get very little out of the Course if that is all we learn. What the Holy Spirit does is remain in our mind, and to that presence of love in our mind, we bring all of the concerns and problems that we have, as we will see in just a minute. The Holy Spirit doesn't do anything with the effects. He doesn't look to the effects because there are no effects.

He remains in our mind, which is the cause, and His love in our mind is the judgment of that cause, which is sin, and the judgment is, it is a joke to think that time can come to circumvent eternity, which means there is no time. We can say the same thing, it is a joke to think that sin can come to disrupt or circumvent God's Love, which means there is no sin. God's Love has never changed. That is what the Holy Spirit's presence is a reminder of.

That is what the Course means when it tells us in many places—probably the clearest statement of that is a passage on page 19 in the teacher's manual, which talks about the function of a teacher of God. And it is talking about it in the context of healing sickness. And it talks about how the teacher of God doesn't heal because of the words he uses or the laying on of hands or any of the kinds of things that the body does. The way the teacher of God heals is by being a reminder of the truth, which is the way that Jesus heals, which is the way the Holy Spirit heals. That we all remain within that place of love and peace, which is a place of certainty in our mind.

Our peace in the presence of someone who's upset stands as the reminder of what the truth is. The truth is, the cause of your upset lies in your mind, and it lies in a thought that has had no effect at all. My love and my presence and my defense-lessness in your presence is the witness to the truth of that thought of the Atonement. That is all that we do. You don't have to do anything. Your body may end up doing something because the love will come through you, as we talked earlier.

But you will not feel the need or the investment in doing anything. We remain within that quiet place of love and peace in our mind and then that love works through us. Our bodies may then become very active, but we will not experience our bodies as doing anything. We will experience the love coming through us. That is why, when you do this right, you don't get tired, you don't get disappointed, you don't get frustrated. That the love comes through you and you literally experience yourself as doing nothing.

The only judgment then that we would make based upon all of this is that the problem is not outside; the problem is inside. Together with Jesus and the Holy Spirit, we judge that inner problem, that inner cause, and we smile at it. And we say, "This has no power to interrupt or destroy or disrupt or distort the love and the peace of God." That is again what this is saying.

(T-27.VIII.9:1) In gentle laughter does the Holy Spirit perceive the cause, and looks not to effects.

That is why, to quote again from that workbook lesson, we can look at sickness, starvation, poverty and death and laugh at it. Because it is the gentle laughter that looks at the cause of all that. The cause is that I am separate from God. We smile at that because we know with certainty that that other person is not separate from God's Love because I am not separate from God's Love. So again:

(T-27.VIII.9:2) How else could He [the Holy Spirit] **correct your error, who have overlooked the cause entirely?**

What our prayer really should be is not that we get a parking space, but that we should be able to accept that love within our mind that will undo the belief in scarcity that has led to the concern for not having a parking space. Because the issue is not whether you get a parking space or not; the issue is whether you remember that there is a parking space for you in Heaven. That is the issue. That is what we want. Not the silly parking space for the car. We want to remember that we did not lose that parking space in Heaven.

That is why people get crazy about parking spaces with the Holy Spirit. They want magically to know that if He gets me the parking space in midtown New York, then that means that I have my parking space in Heaven. And it doesn't work that way. The way it works is that if I ask His help to remind me that I am not alone and I have not lost that parking space in Heaven and I am clear about that, and I feel that love and that certainty and that peace, then whether or not I get the parking space on 42nd Street is irrelevant. I may get it, I may not get it. But it won't matter to me anymore, because I now have what I really want.

When Jesus says in the Course that the problem is not that we ask for too much, but for far too little, that's what he means (W-pI.133.2:1). We ask to be healed of cancer and to be healed of not having a parking space and healed of all the silly things that go on in the body's world. What we really want is the love and the peace of God. That is what we should ask for. That is what all this is talking about. Not that there is anything wrong in asking for a parking space if that is the only way at that moment we can accept God's Love. But what Jesus is telling us, is that is very, very little. And what you really want is not the parking space. What you want is an experience of my love.

(T-27.VIII.9:3) He bids you [meaning the Holy Spirit or Jesus] **bring each terrible effect to Him that you may look together on its foolish cause and laugh with Him a while.**

This line also is extremely important. This is a very, very practical rule of thumb; a very, very practical guiding principle. Jesus is not saying to us that we should deny the terrible things that we are experiencing in the world. He's not telling us to deny our pain and our hurt and our jealousy and our loss and our anger and our disappointment and our depression, etc., etc. What he is saying, rather, is experience all of that, but then recognize that it is not what it seems and bring it to me.

In other words, bring the illusion of your sick and suffering body to the truth that is within your mind, which is where I am. Bring the illusion to the truth. Don't bring me into the illusion. That is why he says very early in the text, don't ask me to take your fear away from you, because I cannot do that. He says rather ask my help in removing the conditions that led to the fear. And the conditions always imply a willingness or a decision to be separate (T-2.VII.4:3-4).

He's saying don't ask me to take the effect of fear away from you, because fear is always of something that we perceive outside of us. He says rather ask my help in removing the conditions of separation that led to the fear, which was a decision you made to separate from me or from the Holy Spirit. That is the problem. That I can help you with. Because he explains that if I did that, I would be tampering with the law of cause and effect, and I would be depreciating the power of your mind to choose; and therefore, I would not be helping you (T-2.VII.1:4).

He's saying don't ask me to get you a parking space, because that is magic. Because I can't get you a parking space. But what I can do is I can remind you of your decision to be separate from your parking space in Heaven, which is the cause of your anxiety here in your car. And by joining with me in your mind, you are rejoining that parking space you believe that you left in Heaven. And that I can help you with.

So again, that is what he's saying. The Holy Spirit is asking us to look at all the things that are bothering us in the world, but to look at them with His love next to us. Which means we bring the pain to Him and we recognize that we are invested in being angry, in being upset, in being sick, in being concerned, because we are afraid of that love. Because we know that if we let go of all those thoughts, that our egos disappear and all that will be left will be that love of God within us.

That is what frightens us. So we choose to be upset by things in the world, the world of effects, as a defense against that love. And then we make all kinds of judgments as if there were things outside of us that were real. When the only judgment we are asked to make is the judgment of the cause, which is to say that this thought of being separate from your love has no power. When I can look at that belief with Jesus next to me, obviously then I am no longer separate from him. So simply by looking with his love, what I am doing is judging that thought of separation and I am now saying, that belief that I could be separate from you has had no effect, and therefore, it is just a silly idea.

(T-27.VIII.9:4) *You* **judge effects, but** *He* **has judged their cause.**

We are the ones who judge all the effects in the world—"This is good; this is bad." He doesn't judge effects. He doesn't even see effects. The Holy Spirit judges the cause, that tiny, mad idea, and says, "Isn't that silly."

(T-27.VIII.9:5) And by His judgment [by the Holy Spirit's judgment that the tiny, mad idea is silly and is only worthy of being laughed at] **are** [all the] **effects removed.**

All the effects of pain, all the effects of fear, all the effects of sin, of guilt, are gone, because I've removed the cause.

(T-27.VIII.9:6) Perhaps you come in tears.

Jesus is not saying to us that this world is a happy place. In fact, he's saying just the opposite. He's not denying the pain and the fear and the sadness and the loneliness and the tears that we feel. But what he is saying is that we can do something to undo the cause of the tears.

(T-27.VIII.9:7) But hear Him say, "My brother, holy Son of God, behold your idle dream, in which this could occur."

What Jesus is asking us to do is when we find ourselves upset by anything in the world, is to step back in our mind and look with him at this dream. If I can step back in my mind and look with Jesus at whatever it is that is upsetting me and causing me pain in any way, shape or form, then obviously, I am beginning the process of separating myself from my ego mind. If I can look with Jesus at my ego, obviously, it is not the ego that I am looking with.

Which means I am already beginning the process and strengthening the process of knowing there is another voice in my mind I can listen to. There is another choice, and there is another presence I can join with. When I join with his presence and look at my ego getting upset, I can begin the process of hearing him say, you know this is not what you think it is. The cause of your pain is not what this body has done to your body, or what this germ has done. The cause of your pain is your belief system. And the dream is an idle dream (T-27.VIII.9:7). It is an idle dream because it doesn't go anywhere.

When a car is idling, it doesn't do anything. When a person is idle, he or she is not working. The ego's dream is an idle dream because nothing happens in the dream. Just as nothing real happens on a puppet stage. Nobody is being killed, nobody is living, nobody is dying, nobody is falling in love, nobody is falling out of love. It is only lifeless pieces of wood that appear to be talking and acting and interacting. In reality, nothing is happening. Well, this whole world is a puppet stage and nothing is happening here. Within the stage, it appears that very real and terrible things happen here, as well as very good things happen here. In reality, nothing is happening here.

When we can step back into that place in our mind which is where the Holy Spirit is or Jesus is, and look with him at what was upsetting us, it means we have been able to begin the process of suspending our investment in believing what is happening to us. That is what the Course refers to as the little willingness. It is the little willingness to look at whatever it is we have invested in, which is always some degree of pain— and as the Course explains, pleasure is the other side of pain. In fact, at one point, Jesus is almost kind of laughing at us, and saying you really believe there is a difference between pleasure and pain. They are opposite sides of the same coin because both of them make the body real.

When we step back with him and look at this, what we are really doing is saying I recognize that I have an investment in being angry. I have an investment in being right. I have an investment in being angry and sad. I have an investment in being victimized. When I can begin to let go of that investment, that is what allows me to look with him on the dream and say, yes, indeed, this is an idle dream. The reason I am upset is not because of what this person has done to me.

The reason I am upset is because I want to be upset. Because I want to justify my judgment that I am separate from God's Love and God is punishing me. If I can prove that there are people suffering out there, I am proving that God is really

71

angry and God is wrathful, God believes in sacrifice, and that the sin against Him is real.

(T-27.VIII.9:7-8) But hear Him say, "My brother, holy Son of God, behold your idle dream, in which this could occur." And you will leave the holy instant [the holy instant being that instant, when we choose to go back to that place in our mind where Jesus is or the Holy Spirit. And you will leave the holy instant] **with your laughter and your brother's joined with His.**

There is another passage in the workbook that talks about how we should leave the world of darkness and for an instant go back to that place of light in our minds. And then go back to the darkness, not because it is real, but to be able to proclaim its unreality in terms and words that the world can understand.

We are not asked to deny this world or what happens in this world. We are simply asked to deny the ego's interpretation of what happens in this world. We go into that place in our mind, that holy instant, and we look at what is really going on, and then we come back into the world, which means our attention is now back in the world, and we laugh at what is happening. And it is not an unfeeling, uncaring, thoughtless laughter. It is a laughter that is filled with compassion and love. It is a laughter that says, don't be upset, nothing has happened.

This doesn't necessarily mean that these are the words that we use. It doesn't mean if a loved one is dying of cancer, you say, "What are you so upset about; nothing is happening?" That is silly, that is cruel; that is not loving. It is talking about a thought that is in your mind that doesn't judge the effect, but simply judges the cause and in our minds, we say, "Behold the idle dream in which this could occur." Nothing is really happening.

I may say the exact same words that someone else in the world may say to you when you are upset and sick. But there will be a peace in my mind and there will be a love in my mind that will not be in that other person who still believes the dream is real. This is the way that Jesus and the Holy Spirit act with us, and this is the way they are asking us to act and be with each other. Not to be upset and not to judge the effects, but to go back into our mind and judge the cause, which is the belief that we are separate from God. And by the love and the peace that we feel, we are saying that cause is not real.

The Cause of Fear

Q: I ride on the New York City subway every day and I experience a great deal of fear all the time. Sometimes all I can do is, in my mind, say I am very frightened, please help. But what is the process beyond that?

A: I think you said it. There is no process beyond that. I think certainly when you are riding on the subway, it is not helpful and it is not practical to be told that you are not a body. But what you can learn is that you can ride on the subways and not be afraid. It doesn't mean you are not prudent and it doesn't mean that you ride in the middle of the night through Harlem and fall asleep on the car. But it does mean that it is possible to be in the subway and be aware of your fear and say to Jesus, I am aware that I am afraid of what might happen to me because I don't feel thoroughly secure in your love. That you can be aware of. And that is all you have to be aware of.

Because if you really felt God's Love with you on the BMT, you would not be afraid. And so the fact that you are afraid is not because you are riding on the BMT. The fact you are afraid is because you believe that you are riding alone on the BMT. All you have to say exactly that, "I am afraid because I feel that I am alone, and I am really afraid of knowing that your love is with me." That is all you do. Because what you are doing is you are bringing the problem from the effect back to the cause.

You are not judging the effect, which is the reason I am upset is because of this subway. That is judging the outside.

What you are judging is the cause. And you are saying, the reason I am upset and afraid is because I believe I am separate from God's Love. That is the cause. You have brought the problem back to where it belongs. That is the right use of judgment. Because there is no attack, obviously, and you are not making the error real. You are saying this is why I am upset—it is because of a thought in my mind.

Then go right on being afraid. Go right on doing all the things that your ego tells you you have to do to survive in New York City. But just be aware that the reason that you are doing this, that you are having to use all of those defenses is because you are afraid of the real cause. The real cause is in your mind and the cause is the denial of God's Love.

Q: The investment in believing that the body is real is important to look, isn't it?

A: Yes, except that that is not very helpful when you feel your body is very real. In other words, please keep in mind this is not a Course in denial. It is not saying to deny the body. Nowhere does the Course ever say that. What it does say is deny the ego's use of the body, but not to deny your physical experience. That never helps. Just be in touch with the fear but call it by its proper name. Label its cause.

The cause of my fear is not what these people may do to me in the car. The cause of my anger is not because the man cut me off on the highway. The cause of my anger, the cause of my fear is because I believe I am separate from God's Love. That is all you have to do. That is what it means to bring the effect to him. That is what Jesus says. Just bring the terrible effects to him.

All things are echoes of the Voice for God (cont.)

Let's go back to where we had stopped in the workbook. We finished with that passage in the text. Nobody likes that passage. We're back in the workbook on page 279.

(W-pI.151.9:1) And thus He judges you.

This actually picks up from the paragraph above it; namely, that the way the Holy Spirit judges us is that He doesn't see any of the illusions. He doesn't see any of the thoughts of the ego. All that He knows is the love of Christ which we are.

(W-pI.151.9:2) Accept His Word for what you are, for He bears witness to your beautiful creation, and the Mind Whose Thought created your reality.

Basically, the Holy Spirit doesn't know from the illusion. He realizes, as the workbook says later on, that what is false is false and what is true has never changed (W-pII.10.1:1). And that the truth of Christ in us has never changed. And all the other thoughts in our split mind are simply illusory.

(W-pI.151.9:3-7) What can the body mean to Him Who knows the glory of the Father and the Son? What whispers of the ego can He hear? What could convince Him that your sins are real? Let Him be Judge as well of everything that seems to happen to you in this world. His lessons will enable you to bridge the gap between illusions and the truth.

I think that that line is extremely important.

(W-pI.151.9:6) Let Him be Judge as well of everything that seems to happen to you in this world.

What seems to happen to us in this world is that things happen to us that take away the love and the peace of Christ that is within us. Things appear to impinge upon us. Things appear to victimize us. Things appear to have an effect on us. And we judge all of these things as having that power. The Holy Spirit's judgment is simply, all that is silly, in the sense that we believe that it can have an effect on us. What other people do, what other people say, what the environment does or does not do— all has no effect on the peace of God in my mind.

The Holy Spirit's judgment of all that, again, is that it is all silly. He does not dismiss the feelings that we have or the experiences that we have. He simply reinterprets them. And helps us to understand that what we believe had an effect on us was really caused by us. That we are the ones who are responsible for all the feelings and the experiences that we have. On a practical level within this dream, this doesn't mean that we are the cause of what other people do.

But we are the cause of what our reactions are to what other people do. And that, again, is what the Holy Spirit's judgment is. That it is not something outside of me that has caused me to be upset or to be distressed. I am the cause of that distress. Once again, it is a total misunderstanding of what the Course is teaching to believe that the Holy Spirit messes with the world and fixes up the world that is outside of us. That would absolutely make no sense in terms of the Atonement plan. What He does is that He recalls our attention from the world back within and helps us recognize that the reason we are upset is because of a decision we have made in our mind. If we bring that decision back to the decision maker, back to His love, and change our mind, then all the pain and misery and distress will disappear.

(W-pI.151.10:1) He will remove all faith that you have placed in pain, disaster, suffering and loss.

What is important here is the idea that we have placed our faith in pain, disaster, suffering and loss, and we have done that because listening to the ego, which is the voice that we have not only listened to but have identified with, and become that thought system, we believe that pain, disaster, suffering, loss and death, save us from God's wrath. There is a workbook lesson later on that says, "I choose the joy of God instead of pain." It talks about in that lesson that if there is pain, there is no God. If there is God, there is no pain (W-pI.190.3:3-4). Both cannot coexist. Pain is only of the body, pain is of the ego; and that cannot coexist with the love of God.

To quote again from John's letters, as I did earlier, and the Course does a few times, "perfect love casts out fear" (T-1.VI.5:4). In a brightened room, you cannot have darkness. Just like in a mind filled with love, you cannot have fear. You also cannot have pain. That is why Jesus did not suffer on the cross. It is only a mind that is filled with guilt that can suffer pain. Since his mind only was filled with the love of God, there was no pain.

Pain is not of the body. Pain is of the mind. Pain is a decision that the mind makes that it then seeks to disguise. It seeks to disguise the fact that it made such a decision, transfers the pain from the mind onto the body, so we now believe that the body is in pain. But as we have seen, the body is nothing more than a puppet. It doesn't feel anything; it doesn't do anything. It is the mind that feels the pain, which is guilt and fear, and transfers that onto the body.

We are the ones who have chosen pain and suffering, because that is what keeps God away. If there is pain, there is no God. It is God that I am afraid of, because the ego tells me if I get into God's clutches, He will punish me and destroy me. So God becomes the enemy. Then the way that I keep God away from me is to keep myself in a body. the way I keep the reality of the body in my mind is to suffer pain. That is one of the more popular and certainly one of the more powerful ways of ensuring that our attention stays riveted on our body.

We all know when we are in pain, whether we are talking about physical pain or psychological pain, that nothing is more real than that pain. It becomes a wonderful distraction device that keeps our attention rooted on our bodies and not in our minds. If God is in our mind and not in our body, then the perfect way to keep God away from us is to stay in pain and stay in suffering, and to have that investment. That is why this is written that way.

We have placed our faith in pain and suffering and death because that is what the ego tells us will insure our survival, which it certainly does as an ego. It doesn't make us very happy, but within the ego system it certainly keeps us alive. What we have to learn is that we should put our faith in miracles; we should put our faith in forgiveness. We should put our faith in the love that is present in our mind, not in the pain and suffering of our bodies.

So again, what the Holy Spirit does is simply recall our attention from what is outside of us. He helps us recognize that pain is not of the body, loss is not of the body, and love is not of the body. That pain and loss are thoughts within our mind, just as love is a thought within our mind. That is how the Holy Spirit heals. He helps us bring the illusion back to the truth within, and then the problem disappears.

Q: You talked about what to do about fear, for example, on the subway system. Could you use that same mode to talk about what you do when you are in the midst of pain in the body? How you can at that moment transfer that back?

A: I think when you have pain in the body, that the principle is exactly the same as when you are riding in the subway. When you have pain in the body, you say obviously I am afraid of God's Love because I've chosen to be in pain. And obviously, that is what my ego does, and so what else is new. And you take whatever painkiller works for you or do whatever magic works for you. Just be aware that what you are doing is that you are trying to keep God's Love away from you because you are afraid of it.

But the fact that you can be aware of it is very, very healing. That is all you do. You don't make a big deal about it. You don't say a good *Course in Miracles* student doesn't go to a doctor. That is silly. In fact, what will probably make you a good *Course in Miracles* student is to go to a doctor, but not to take it seriously and not to make a big deal about it. So yes, the same principle would hold.

(W-pI.151.10:2) He gives you vision which can look beyond these grim appearances, and can behold the gentle face of Christ in all of them.

78

So once again, Jesus is not denying the grim appearances that seem real to us in this world. Just as we talked earlier, that he does not deny the heavy consequences of sin that appear to be so real here. All he's telling us is that it is not what you think it is. If you look to the cause, which is in your mind and you judge the cause instead of the effect, then the pain of the effect will disappear.

(W-pI.151.10:3) You will no longer doubt that only good can come to you who are beloved of God, for He will judge all happenings, and teach the single lesson that they all contain.

This should not be taken to mean that if you do the Holy Spirit's lessons or you are a good *Course in Miracles* student that good will come to you on the level of form. This doesn't mean that at all. Because you can do the Holy Spirit's lessons beginning in Auschwitz and end up in Auschwitz and nothing has changed, and no good has come of that on the level of form, but something has been transformed within you. What earlier was looked on as a battleground and as a place of death will now be seen as a lovely classroom in which you've learned the only lesson that anyone has to learn; namely, that God's Love is all that there is. And nothing outside of me has the power to take that love away from me.

When it says only good can come to you, it doesn't mean good on a material basis. Often, people work with the Course and they believe if I do this course, then only good things will happen. I'll make a lot of money, I'll be healed of AIDS and healed of cancer and all these wonderful people will come into my life, etc., etc. What that does very subtly is make the error real, and confuses form with content. It doesn't mean good things may not happen to you on the level of form, but that is not a criterion for evaluating your success with the Course.

The criterion would be that no matter what happens, I am still at peace. My investment is not in having the outside world change, but rather my investment is in learning that there is no outside world. Otherwise, you get caught in the same kinds of judgment that everyone else gets caught in. And then it becomes the old Calvinist argument, just kind of sifted through new age language, and that is, I know that I am a good person, I know that God loves me because all good things are happening to me. And if bad things happen, then it means I am not doing my *Course in Miracles* lessons properly. And that is not what this is talking about.

What the Course helps us realize is that regardless of what happens in the world, the love of God is still within me. And again, that is what the message of the crucifixion was. No matter what happened to the body of Jesus, the love of God in him was not changed. These words are a very good example to use in terms of this kind of thinking. Because nothing very good happened in his life, certainly in the world of form. He says a few times in the Course that we should take him as our model for learning. The model is that even though things around him did not work out all that favorably in the eyes of most people in the world, that the love and the peace within him was totally unaffected. Therefore it does not matter what happens to you. This doesn't mean things have to get worse and it doesn't mean everyone has to be crucified in order to learn lessons. All that it means is that it doesn't matter.

(W-pI.151.11:1-2) He will select the elements in them which represent the truth, and disregard those aspects which reflect but idle dreams. And He will reinterpret all you see, and all occurrences, each circumstance, and every happening that seems to touch on you in any way from His one frame of reference, wholly unified and sure.

This actually is the answer to the question Allen had raised earlier of that passage in lesson 135. This is really what the Holy Spirit does. He doesn't change the occurrences. He doesn't change the happenings. He doesn't change the events in our lives. He reinterprets what we see. That is what all this is about. What a miracle is, is a shift in perception. It is a reinterpretation of what we have made real. It is a different judgment. It is a different way of looking; it is a different way of thinking.

It has nothing to do with anything external. That is why, again, the Holy Spirit doesn't do anything or manipulate anything in the world. His one judgment in all things is basically that there is another way of looking at this. Our way of looking at it is, "Isn't this awful? Or isn't this wonderful?" And the "this" always refers to something in the world of form, something that involves bodies. The Holy Spirit's interpretation is that this is not wonderful and this is not awful. All that it is, is a classroom, a neutral screen, a blank screen onto which you have projected your inner thoughts, which are ones of sacrifice and fear and loss. If you listen to me, I can show you how this can then be used to heal those thoughts. That is what the miracle does.

Q: To talk about this in the context of my videotape library, my script, is it possible that in one of my videotapes, I am problem free? That there would be no things that break down? No plumbing problems? Those kinds of things? Is that possible?

A: Yeah, sure. Except maybe that is not the best way of learning lessons. Maybe the best way of learning lessons is to have breakdowns like that so you can learn that it doesn't make any difference. It doesn't mean you don't fix them. But you can fix them with peace or you can fix them with anger and resentment and conflict and tension and fear. The lesson is how to deal with all the practical problems with peace. If everything goes absolutely perfectly, then the chances are, you are not going to learn anything. Except probably to get smug and arrogant.

The idea, again, which really makes the point I think very, very clearly, is that we always judge according to form. We always judge by what the body tells us, which is what we saw in the first part of this workbook lesson. I know I am doing well because of something external going a certain way. I must be doing poorly because I ended up in a concentration camp. That is absurd. I know I am doing poorly because of all these problems that are happening in my life. The only criterion that we should ever use to evaluate how we are doing—is the degree of peace that we have. The lesson would be that we can be at peace regardless of what is happening around us.

(W-pI.151.11:3) And you will see the love beyond the hate, the constancy in change, the pure in sin, and only Heaven's blessing on the world.

What this means is that when we let the Holy Spirit look through us, when we bring our concerns, our anxieties, our angers, our judgments, to His love (in other words, we go from the darkness where we believe we are to the light that is in our mind), then our mind is quiet and we have released all our judgments. Then we go back and pay attention to the darkness, and we will see everything differently. Then we will see exactly what is talked about here—the love beyond the hate, the constancy in change, etc. The world of form doesn't change. What changes is the way that we look at it. We realize, as we will see a little bit later on, that the only judgment the Holy Spirit makes is either someone is expressing God's Love or calling for it.

A behavior that the world judges as hateful or as sinful will be reinterpreted by the love in our mind as being an expression of fear, and fear is a call for the love of God that has been denied, and that we don't feel we deserve. That is the perception or the vision Jesus had from the cross. He did not deny what the bodies were doing, but he certainly gave a different interpretation to it.

When it talks about the constancy in change, this is another way of understanding why Jesus tells us repeatedly how very simple his Course is. It is simple because everything is the same. Regardless of what you do, I perceive you in the same way. That is the constancy in change. The world is always changing. People's behavior is always changing. People's words are always changing, the weather is always changing. Bodies are always changing. Everything is always changing; that is what the world is. But it is possible to have a constancy in vision.

If everything in the world is either an expression of love or a call for love, it makes my behavior and my response very, very easy. If you are my brother or sister in Christ, and you are expressing God's Love to me, then my response would always be one of love. If you are my brother and sister in Christ and you are calling for God's Love, then my response as your loving brother would be to extend that love to you, which means regardless of what you do, my response is always identical. Whether you are calling for love or expressing love, my response will always be loving, which means I don't even have to know what you are doing, whether you are calling for love or expressing love. Because my response will always be the same. That is the constancy. Even though the outer world is always changing, my mind can always be rooted in the love of God.

What is helpful, then, is to be in touch with how complex we make everything. And how we have set up for ourselves a complex series of laws and rules to govern the way that we react. If you act a certain way towards me, I will act a certain way back. If you act a different way towards me, I'll act a different way. At times it can get rather intricate and rather subtle, but we always modify our behaviors and our reactions based upon how other people treat us or other people treat other people whom we identify with. It makes everything very complicated.

This makes everything very, very simple. No matter what you do, I still perceive the same Christ in you. No matter what you do, it doesn't change the love within me for you. And despite however hateful your behavior may be as judged by the world, I will still see it as a call for love.

I will realize that everything that you are doing in terms of the ego is your attempt to keep the love of God that is within your mind away from you. Making the same judgment as the Holy Spirit does, I will say that all of your attempts are simply silly, no matter how awful they appear. That all of your attempts, whether it is on the scale of a Hitler or the scale of somebody who just kind of plays a foolish prank on somebody else that is not very loving (no matter what it is), I will realize this is just a silly attempt on your ego's part to keep the love of God away from you. That is the judgment that I make.

I don't judge your behavior. I judge the whole thought system that you are espousing. Again, that is exactly what the Holy Spirit does. As we saw earlier, He doesn't judge the effects. He judges the cause. The cause, which is sin or the tiny, mad idea, He judges as merely being silly. That is the same judgment He would have us make. So no matter what you do; again, no matter how heinous a crime it may be in the eyes of the world, I would still see it as just a silly and flimsy little veil that is your attempt to keep the love of God away from you because you are afraid of it. And that is all that I would see. And that is how we see love in hate and that is how we see constancy in change and purity in sin.

(W-pI.151.12:1) Such is your resurrection, for your life is not a part of anything you see.

This was written shortly after Easter. That is why it has the resurrection idea there. And resurrection in the Course obviously has nothing whatsoever to do with the body. What resurrection is, is the awakening from the dream of death. It is the acceptance of the Atonement for one's self. It is choosing to identify only with the Holy Spirit and not with the ego. That is what resurrection is. If crucifixion is a dream of pain and suffering and injustice and death, then resurrection is the undoing or the awakening from that dream.

(W-pI.151.12:1) … for your life is not a part of anything you see.

What is it that I see? I see bodies. I see a world. I see form. I see change; I see death; I see pain, etc., etc., etc. My life is not a part of that because my life is not of my body. We would say not only is the resurrection the awakening from the dream of death, it is also an awakening from the dream of the body, because obviously it is only a body that can die. This is another way of understanding what Jesus was teaching us from the cross. He was saying my life is not a part of anything that you see. What you are seeing is my dying and crucified body. That is what you are seeing. That is not who I am. But not only is it not who I am, it is also not who you are.

(W-pI.151.12:2) It stands beyond the body [the "it" of course here is life. Life stands beyond the body] **and the world, past every witness for unholiness, within the Holy, holy as Itself.**

The Holy is capitalized because that refers to God. Our life is not of the body. There is a passage in "The Laws of Chaos" section that says that "there is no life outside of Heaven" (T-23.II.19:1). That is meant to be taken literally. There is no life outside of Heaven. And then it goes on, everything that is outside of Heaven is not alive. There is no life there, which means everything in this world is not alive. It is also not dead. It simply is nonexistent. If you say something is dead, the implication is that it was once alive. There is no life in this world; there is no life in this body.

That is why all the judgments that are made in this world, whether they are the judgments that society approves of or those that society condemns, are all based upon the fact that there is something real here, and the body is real. If I am a murderer, I believe that I am justified in taking your life, because unconsciously, I believe you took my life.

That is that battle that originated with God. I believe God stole my life; I steal it back from Him. Now I am afraid He's going to steal it back. And we go back and forth. And either He's alive or I am alive but we both can't be alive and coexist. That is the thought that gets projected into the world. We therefore believe people have stolen things from us and we are justified in stealing them back.

Or we put a value on human life and a premium on human life. We feel it is our job to save human life or prolong human life, or stop other people from taking human life or animal life or plant life or whatever. We want to save the trees or save the whales or save the planet or save the aborted fetuses or whatever. We are always trying to save something that wasn't alive in the first place. So again, those are the judgments that we make. We judge what is alive and what is not alive. Nothing in this world is alive. The only life that exists is the life of spirit which is in Heaven: the life of Christ and the life of God, and there is nothing else.

(W-pI.151.12:3-4) In everyone and everything His Voice would speak to you of nothing but your Self and your Creator, Who is one with Him. So will you see the holy face of Christ in everything, and hear in everything no sound except the echo of God's Voice.

That of course is what the theme of the lesson is—"All things are echoes of the Voice for God." This does not mean that God's Voice speaks to me from a tree or from another person. What it means is, is that since God's Voice is in my mind and my mind has projected out an experience of a tree or an experience of another person, and that thought is within my mind, since ideas leave not their source, then the voice of the Holy Spirit speaks to me through the projection that I have made.

It would be the same thing, if I am watching a movie, and somebody puts a black dot on the film, that black dot will then be perceived on the screen. But it is not on the screen; it is in the film. Just as if I am watching the same film and somebody puts a white dot—so the black dot would be the ego and the white dot would be the Holy Spirit—on the film. The white dot will show up on the screen. There is no white dot on the screen; the white dot is in the film. Similarly, the Holy Spirit's Voice is in my mind, which is the film. The ego's voice is in my mind, which is in the film. It is not on the screen.

When the workbook lesson says, "God is in everything I see" (W-pI.29) and the subsequent lesson is, "God is in everything I see because God is in my mind" (W-pI.30) that is not a statement of Pantheism. It is not saying God is in what I perceive. It is not in that chair; it is not in that person; it is not in the lake. Because there is nothing out there, just as there is nothing in a movie screen.

God is in everything I see because God is in my mind. So again, if there is a voice of love in my mind, that is what I will project out and perceive outside of me as if it were outside of me. If there is guilt that I choose in my mind and that is in my film, that is what I will project and see outside of me. This doesn't mean that God's Voice speaks to me from what is outside. There is nothing outside. God's Voice speaks to me from within. But because I have made the mistake of taking what is within and putting it without, then that love, which is also within my mind, will also be experienced without; in other words, outside of me.

When the Course says here, as it says on the top of the page, "So will you see the holy face of Christ in everything" (W-pI.151.12:4), it is not talking about literally perceiving a face in somebody else. It is certainly not talking about seeing the face of Jesus in anyone. To see the face of Christ is talking about an inner experience. It is talking about an attitude. To see the face of Christ in you simply means I see the innocence in you because I am recognizing the same innocence that is in myself. It doesn't mean that your physical body changes. It doesn't mean that I perceive you differently.

When the Course talks about seeing light in people, it doesn't mean that you physically see light. Some people may have those experiences, but if you have that kind of experience, that is simply a symbol for what is within you. What it is talking about is there is an attitude of light in your mind that you have identified with. There is a thought of light in your mind. And just as, once again, if you have something on a film, that is what you'll see on the screen. If there is light in my mind, that is what I will perceive outside of me on the movie screen. But it is not there. Just as everyone knows, there are not people running around on a movie screen. That is an illusion. Well, it is the same thing here; that there aren't people running around outside of me. That is an illusion. The way that I perceive you is telling me the way that I perceive me.

When the Course talks about seeing the face of Christ in someone, or hearing God's Voice in everything, it does not mean literally hearing God's Voice from outside. Because we have the illusion of being outside of our mind, we will have the illusion of hearing God's Voice outside of our mind. Because we have the illusion of being outside of our mind, we will have the illusion of seeing Christ's face outside of our mind. But that is not what this is talking about.

The Course is never, ever talking about anything external. Never. You can just take that as a given. Nothing that it says in terms of the Holy Spirit's teachings have anything to do with the external world because there is no external world. It only has to do with our perceptions or our thoughts about the external world. Again, as I quoted earlier, that is why that line is so important: Therefore, seek not to change the world, but choose to change your mind about the world (T-21.in.1:7). It makes no point to change a world outside of you when there is nothing outside of you.

It does make sense to change your mind about what you believed was outside of you. Because the whole problem was, we believed our mind changed right at the beginning. That we changed from being part of God's Mind to being part of the ego's mind. That was the first change. Because of that change, we have to change back to remembering that we are still part of God's Mind. But you don't change what is outside because there is nothing outside.

The idea again is that when I choose to let the Holy Spirit look through me, and I make the judgment that is His judgment; namely, that there is nothing outside of me that has any power over me or anybody else—and that the cause of everything that is perceived outside is within and it is a cause that is silly—and that is again what the judgment is—then I do see the innocence of Christ in everyone, because I've accepted the innocence of Christ within myself. I do hear God's Voice speak in everything and from everything because that is the only Voice I am hearing inside of me.

(W-pI.151.13) We practice wordlessly today, except at the beginning of the time we spend with God. [This actually has to do with what we are supposed to do with the meditation.] **We introduce these times with but a single, slow repeating of the thought with which the day begins. And then we watch our thoughts, appealing silently to Him Who sees the elements of truth in them.** [The elements of truth in our thoughts are the elements that reflect the love of God that is within. Whether I am expressing that love or I am calling for it.] **Let Him** [meaning the Holy Spirit] **evaluate each thought that comes to mind, remove the elements of dreams, and give them back again as clean ideas that do not contradict the Will of God.**

In this world, in which the Will of God is not expressed, we can be a reflection of that Will and not contradict that Will. If God's Will is perfect unity, which is impossible in this world, we are yet able within the illusion to have a thought that you and I are not separate. That thought, then, does not contradict God's Will. It is not God's Will because there cannot be a Will of God in a place that doesn't exist. But it is possible in this world to have no thoughts that contradict God's Will.

That is what the Course means by true perception or the real world. That no thought that we have here contradicts the love and the unity of God, which means those thoughts would include thoughts of love, thoughts of peace, thoughts of healing, thoughts of joining, thoughts of forgiveness. So then again, what we are asked to do is to watch our thoughts. At this point, it sounds very Buddhist. We are asked to watch our thoughts because that is all that there is.

But we are asked to watch our thoughts, not with our ego, but with the Holy Spirit. Again, that is why the Course places such a strong emphasis on simply looking at our ego. And if I look at my ego, I am no longer looking at it with my ego; I am looking at my ego with the Holy Spirit or with Jesus beside me. At that point, then, I look at my thoughts of anger, my thoughts of sickness, my thoughts of murder, my thoughts of rage, my thoughts of disappointment, my thoughts of depression, my thoughts of guilt, on and on—and I look at them with the Holy Spirit next to me. And together with Him, I laugh at the silliness of believing that any of those thoughts has the power to take God's Love away from me. That is what the judgment of the Holy Spirit really is. And that is what we are asked to do. Not to deny the angry thoughts or ego thoughts we have, but to bring them to that love that is also a thought in our mind. And together with that thought, with that presence of Jesus or the Holy Spirit, I look back on my ego thoughts and I smile at them.

Using Jim's example again, when you are driving down the road and somebody cuts you off, you don't deny your anger, you don't deny your rage, you don't deny that you are a victim. What you do is you look at the thought, you just watch the thought with the love of Jesus with you, and at some point, you look at it and you say this is really silly. What difference does it make that this guy cut me off? What difference does it make, when I can have instead the love and the peace of God?

Even if you are still angry, you can still say, obviously it does make a difference to me. And obviously, I am afraid of that love and peace. But thank God I finally understand why it is I am so angry, why it is I am so miserable, why it is I am so guilty, why it is I am so critical of other people, why it is I am so depressed all the time. It is not for any of the reasons I thought. It is simply because I am afraid of being happy, loving and peaceful. At least now I know what the cause is.

That is how the Holy Spirit's Voice speaks to me in everything that happens. If I find myself getting upset by anything and I let His Voice speak to me, it will tell me I am never upset for the reason I think, which is an early lesson in the workbook (W-pI.5). I am never upset for the reason I think, meaning I am not upset because of what you've done to me. I am upset because I believe I've separated myself from God. At least I now know what the cause is. I may not be at the point yet when I am willing to change it, but I at least know what the problem is, which puts me way, way ahead of the game.

(W-pI.151.14:1) Give Him your thoughts, and He will give them back as miracles which joyously proclaim the wholeness and the happiness God wills His Son, as proof of His eternal Love.

All that we are asked to do is not to not have the thoughts; we are not asked not to have those thoughts. In fact, let me read something from the text which is extremely important. It is on page 311 in the textbook at the bottom of the page.

(T-15.V.9:1-2) The necessary condition for the holy instant does not require that you have no thoughts that are not pure. But it does require that you have none that you would keep.

This is extremely important. Jesus is not saying to us you must be without guilt or be without anger. In fact, earlier in the text, he says you are not guiltless in time, but only in eternity. He's not telling us not to have ego thoughts. He's simply saying, don't hold them back from me. Because if you hold them back from me, you will experience pain and misery and guilt and conflict and depression. Have the thoughts. Have whatever thoughts are there. Don't evaluate them; don't judge them. Simply bring them to me. So again, the only requirement is that you have no thoughts that you would keep. That is what this is talking about.

(W-pI.151.14:1) Give Him your thoughts, and He will give them back as miracles...

Q: How do you give your thoughts?

A: You simply step back and say, "Oh, I am really angry."

Q: And that's the giving of it?

A: Yes, the giving is always simply looking at it without justifying it. So again, if you are driving down the road and somebody cuts you off and you get angry, don't stop getting angry. Simply say, "Oh, I am angry and I think I am angry because the guy cut me off." The real reason I am angry is because I am afraid of God's Love. Whatever words you want to use; it doesn't matter. That is all you do. You simply stop justifying.

(W-pI.151.14:2) And as each thought is thus transformed, it takes on healing power from the Mind which saw the truth in it, and failed to be deceived by what was falsely added.

What was falsely added is the ego's interpretation. The reason I am upset is because this driver victimized me; he cut me off. Well, that's added onto it. That is an interpretation that was added onto it. That becomes a cover for the Holy Spirit's interpretation which simply says, nothing happened. So the guy cut you off? What does that have to do with your mind? That again is what Jesus was teaching. So a group of people crucified me. What does that have to do with my mind? What does that have to do with anything?

That is the way of learning the ultimate lesson that to the tiny, mad idea that we believe had such power to destroy God, the Holy Spirit says, "What does that thought have to do with anything?" Absolutely nothing. That is what we are taught to do in the Course with everything. Again, that is the only judgment we are ever asked to make. What does this have to do with anything? It has a lot to do with bodies. But if I am not a body, what does this have to do with anything?

(W-pI.151.14:3) All threads of fantasy are gone.

Fantasies all have to do with some expression of fulfillment of the ego's wishes. Freud was 100 percent correct. I either have fantasies of having my wishes fulfilled that give me pleasure, or I have fantasies of having my wishes fulfilled that is going to give somebody else pain. Or sometimes people have fantasies of inflicting pain on themselves. But they all have to do with bodies.

(W-pI.151.14:4) And what remains is unified into a perfect Thought that offers its perfection everywhere.

The perfect Thought is God's Love, which in this world is expressed in terms of forgiveness.

The Equality of Miracles

Before we actually go to the manual, I want to look at something in the text on page 294. This is a passage that I've been referring to. This comes near the end of chapter 14. At the beginning of chapter 12 is a section called "The Judgment of the Holy Spirit." We're not going to do that section. But in that section, it talks about the Holy Spirit's judgment that someone is either expressing love or calling for it. What we are going to find here is a bringing back of that theme and kind of extending it somewhat. And I'll start reading at the very bottom of page 294, the last two lines.

(T-14.X.7:1) The only judgment involved is the Holy Spirit's one division into two categories; one of love, and the other the call for love.

That is the only judgment that the Holy Spirit makes of anything or anyone in this world. That a person is either calling for love or expressing love. Once again, it doesn't make any difference, because whether you are calling for love or expressing love, my response will be loving. That is the Holy Spirit's judgment. Everything in this world shares that content; either love or the call for love.

A little later on, it's going to talk about form and content. Judgment from the ego's point of view is always based on form. There are good forms; there are bad forms. The teacher's manual makes the same point. Everything we judge is based on form. Something is good; something is bad. Someone is good; someone is bad. A body is sick; a body is well. And on and on and on. There are good things that happen to me; there are bad things that happen to me. And I believe I know what the differences are.

That is the same idea as in that line I mentioned earlier, that Jesus pokes fun at us and says you really that there is a difference between pleasure and pain (T-27.VI.1). Similarly, we think that there is a difference between good and bad in this world. There are good events, there are bad events; there are good people and there are bad people. Those are our judgments. The truth is that everyone is the same, and people either call for love or express love. And that is the only judgment. That idea that people either call for love or express love is based on content, not on form. We always evaluate on form.

(T-14.X.7:2) You [meaning all of us] **cannot safely make this division,** [between expressions of love and calls for love] **for you are much to confused either to recognize love, or to believe that everything else is nothing but a call for love.**

The reason we are confused is because we have listened to the ego voice, which is a voice that is predicated upon differences. That is why that idea is so important that I began with last night. The whole thought system of the ego begins with the perception of differences. God and His Son are different. And that is where the first judgment came.

We all identified with the ego, which we know, because we all believe we are a body, which again is the embodiment of the ego itself. Because of that, we are totally confused because we believe that differences are reality. The beginning difference between God and His Son has been made real. One is good and one is bad. One has power, one does not have power. One is the Creator; the other is not. Then we steal back and forth from each other within the dream. Who has life and who has love and who has the power? Who, in fact, is God?

Because we believe in differences and that is what truth is, then we will always see differences around us. Following the dictates of the ego, we will see differences in form. The form is what is real. There is good and there is bad. And again, this does not mean that we shouldn't have preferences. Everybody has preferences. We have favorite colors and we have favorite people and we have favorite works of art and we have favorite places to live in and favorite climates and favorite spiritual paths and favorite this and favorite that. The Course is not saying at any point to give up preferences. All Jesus would say is don't make a big deal about them. And don't use your preference as a weapon against yourself or anybody else.

(T-14.X.7:3) You are too bound to form, and not to content.

There is probably no more important theme in the whole Course than this one of the distinction between form and content. It is at the heart of the Course's discussions on special relationships and on the laws of chaos. The ego always judges by form. In fact, everything is form to the ego. That is why the ego made up this world. It made up the world, which is a world of form, as a way of disguising its underlying content.

It never wants us to look at content, because content is purpose. The ego never wants us to understand what its purpose is. Its purpose is always to separate, to exclude, to attack and finally, to kill. That is the ego's purpose. It never lets us see that. It conceals the purpose, it conceals its content, it conceals itself, in the form.

The world was not only made as a place to exclude God's love, it was also made as a place to exclude the ego's guilt and yet to always express it. In other words, that guilt is always expressed in this world, except we don't know it. I am quite clear about your guilt and your sinfulness, but I am always trying to hide my own.

The ego makes the content of guilt and the content of judgment and the content of difference very real. Then it seeks to hide it in the world of form. One of the best expressions of this in the Course is in the section called "The Two Pictures," which is one of the more important sections on special relationships (T-17.IV). It contrasts, as it frequently does, the ego with the Holy Spirit. And it talks about the ego's picture and the Holy Spirit's picture. The ego's picture, which is its content, is death, and then all the words and ideas that are associated with death—guilt, suffering, pain, loss, judgment, etc.

But what the ego does is take its picture of death and hides it, and puts it in a very beautiful and ornate frame, that glitters with all kinds of fancy jewelry. It glitters so much that we don't see the picture. We only see the form. We see this beautiful frame, very heavily elaborated and ornamented, which again glitters with all kinds of fancy jewelry. And obviously, we are attracted to the frame; we are attracted to the form. That is what special relationships are. We are attracted to the other person's body, whether it is the physical body, the psychological body, the size of the person's bank account, whatever it is.

We are attracted to the other person for what that person can do for us.

We are not aware of what the gift really is that we are receiving, which is the gift of guilt, a gift of separation, the gift of the ego, which ends up being a gift in death. But we don't see the content because we are so attracted to the form. And we make judgments based upon form. I want to be with you because I like your picture frame better than *your* picture frame. As if it made a difference. And therefore, I believe the light of Christ is going to shine in you. Of course, it really is not the light of Christ. It is the light of the ego's "christ." It shines in you because you are going to give me what I want. It doesn't shine in the other person because that person will not give me what I want.

The whole point of that section, Jesus says, "Look at the *picture*" not the frame (T-17.IV.9:1). Because it is the picture that is the gift. And it is not a very nice gift. It explains, when we are finally able to look at all this and get close up to the frame, then we realize that the diamonds that glittered from the frame were not diamonds but tears. And that the rubies were not jewelry at all, but they were drops of blood (T-17.IV.8:4). But when you don't look closely at the form, and you just take it for what appears to be its reality, then we become attracted to it.

That is why in this passage here, Jesus is talking about that we always judge based on form and not content. The ego never wants us to judge the content. If we really knew what the ego was up to, we would never pay attention to it. The ego tells us not that we are going to be protected from God's Love. What the ego tells us is, you are going to be protected from God's hatred. And we never question that. And we just go along listening to the ego and saying, "Yes, I must do what you tell me, because if I get too close to love, it will destroy me."

That is why there is a sentence in the workbook that says, "You think you are destroyed, but you are saved" (W-pI.93.4:4).

By identifying with love, we will not be destroyed. We will truly be saved. But there is that nagging little voice inside of me that I still believe is the only voice, that says if you get too close to love it will destroy you. Therefore, you need a defense against that love, which is what the special relationship is. I then identify with the ego's specialness instead of the real love of the Holy Spirit.

The ego never tells us what it is up to. It never tells us its true content. Its purpose is to always keep us in a heightened state of fear—the fear of God's wrath and God's punishment. It doesn't tell us that, because if it told us that, we would never pay attention to it. The ego tells us, listen to me and I will help you decrease fear. So the ego always keeps us somewhat fearful, but never in a state of sheer terror. Because if we were in a state of sheer terror, we would never listen to the ego again. The ego's content, the ego's purpose, is always kept hidden. Its purpose and its content is always death, guilt, fear, pain, etc.

On the other side, the other picture, is a picture of light. That is the light of Christ that shines in us. That is the Holy Spirit's picture. That is what His love reminds us of. That picture is put in a very loose frame. That frame is the body, but it is the Holy Spirit's purpose for the body, not the ego's purpose. The body, which is the separating device that seems to keep us separate and different from each other fades away. It doesn't mean that it literally fades away and that I no longer physically perceive it. It fades away in the sense that it doesn't make any difference to me what your skin color is, what place you came from, what you believe in, what your size is, what your sex is, what your weight is. It doesn't matter to me what your form looks like.

All that matters to me is that you and I are both one. That the picture frame is very light and fades away and is swept up in the light of Christ which is the picture. In other words, the Holy Spirit's picture is the content of God's Love and the light of Christ. And that content is expressed through the form but is not hidden by the form. In other words, I am not taken in by what your body does.

My ego is certainly taken in and always has me judge what your body does and attack you for it. It either comes in the form of a direct attack, which is special hate, or it comes in the form of an indirect attack, which is special love. I love you only for what you can do for me. I don't really love you. I simply love what your ego or your body is going to do for me. The ego's form then hides its content. I really believe that by cannibalizing you and stealing from you and attacking you and smothering you and making love bargains with you, I am going to be better off.

I don't really know that what I am really getting in all of this is the ego's thought system of death and misery and pain and depression and guilt. Because the form has blinded me. The form of getting what I want, of having my needs met, which is what all of my judgments are based upon—how I can have my needs best met—that blinds me to what the ego's gift really is. To the ego, form always conceals content. And that is why all of my judgments are based upon form. The ego never lets me look at its content. Because if I did, I would then make the Holy Spirit's judgment, which is, "Isn't this silly?" The ego never lets me look at its content because if I did, I would be looking at it with the Holy Spirit, and I would simply judge against it as being a silly, tiny, mad idea that has no effect.

But form hides the content, and therefore we always judge upon form. There is good form and there is bad form; there are good people and bad people. The Holy Spirit's judgment is that the form doesn't matter. The form is simply a veil that the ego used to hide the truth. But now the perception of the form, when it is turned over to the Holy Spirit, becomes a means of helping us realize that the form does not have the power to conceal the truth at all. The Holy Spirit's form, which is His perception of the body, simply acts as a thin veil that no longer can conceal the love and the light of Christ that shines in each of us. The form disappears into the content, in terms of the Holy Spirit. In terms of the ego, the form conceals the content.

We will turn back now to 294, the third line.

(T-14.X.7:3) You are too bound to form, and not to content.

That, of course, is why we are so confused. The reason, once again, we are bound to form and not to content, is we are listening to the ego. My ego has told me I will be safe from the terrifying wrath of God if I hide in my body. And the body is form. And so I make this world real, I make this body real and I am always trying to do things to change the world of bodies, whether it is my body or your body. I don't pay attention to the ego's content. Again, the ego uses form to deny and hide content.

The Holy Spirit uses form to express content. That is what it means in the section earlier in the text that talks about the body as a means of communication (T-.6.V.A.5:5). That is the idea of the passage I quoted from last night that Jesus says to us, "I need your voice, I need your eyes, your feet, through which I save the world" (W-pI.r.9:3). Your body, then, will become an instrument that will reflect my love, rather than having your body become an instrument that hides my love, which is what we all do.

(T-14.X.7:4-6) What you consider content is not content at all. It is merely form, and nothing else. [The underlying content of guilt is never looked at. That is what this is talking about.] **For you do not respond to what a brother really offers you, but only to the particular perception of his offering by which the ego judges it.**

In other words, I don't respond to the content of love that you really offer me. Because even if you are attacking me and maligning me and abusing me, you are still offering me love as long as I interpret your seeming attack, as long as I interpret your behavior, as a call for the love of God that you don't believe you deserve. If I look at you through the eyes of the Holy Spirit, I only perceive your offering of love.

Through the eyes of the ego, I judge what you are doing and I say, this is not acceptable to me. And I don't like what you are doing, which obviously means I don't like you. Or I do like what you are doing, because you are stroking me and you are giving me everything that I believe I need. Therefore, I do like you and you can stay now with me. The way that I evaluate you is only by a judgment that the ego sets up. Remember, the ego always judges form. And form to the ego is always based upon differences.

(T-14.X.8:1) The ego is incapable of understanding content, and is totally unconcerned with it.

The only content the ego is concerned with, of course, is guilt, but it never pays any attention to it because it always tells us to hide it, and to hide it in the form.

(T-14.X.8:2-3) To the ego, if the form is acceptable the content must be. [In other words, the ego's content of love is I like you if your form meets my needs.] **Otherwise it will attack the form.**

At this point in the Course, Jesus has not begun to talk about special relationships yet. This is what he's talking about, but he's not labeling it that. If your form is acceptable to me, that is special love. If your form is not acceptable to me, that is special hate and I will attack the form.

(T-14.X.8:4-5) If you believe you understand something of the "dynamics" of the ego, let me assure you that you understand nothing of it. [There are a lot of humbling lines in this book.] **For of yourself you could not understand it.**

Because the self that this is talking about is the ego self. The ego cannot understand itself because it doesn't allow us to really look at it. The only way we can understand the dynamics of the ego is through the Holy Spirit, Who teaches us that there is nothing to understand about the ego, because to understand something means that it is real. The only thing there is to understand about the ego is that the whole thing is made up.

(T-14.X.8:6-8) The study of the ego is not the study of the mind. In fact, the ego enjoys studying itself, and thoroughly approves the undertakings of students who would "analyze" it, thus approving its importance. Yet they but study form with meaningless content.

What this is talking about is people trying to understand this world, understand the body, understand the brain. That is what it means here when he says, "The study of the ego is not the study of the mind." What he means by studying the ego is what we all do; we study the body. We study the thought systems that the ego has made up. We spend tremendous time and effort both individually as well as collectively as a society trying to understand the ego's world. We try to understand it from a psychological point of view, from a chemical point of view, a biological point of view, a physiological point of view, a sociological point of view, a political point of view.

Q: Astrological?

A: I left that out. You would feel I was attacking you. But since you brought it up, we try to understand it from an astrological point of view. We try to study the world from all different points of view. And we feel well, we are getting closer and closer. Now I really understand how the body works. Now I really understand how disease works. And then what the ego does is throw up another disease that we never heard of. We just keep going on and on studying what the ego is, which literally is studying nothing. Because the whole thing, again, is just a hall of mirrors. There is nothing there.

A wonderful example of all of this is the children's story of *The Emperor's New Clothes*. The emperor has no clothes. But nobody says it. Everybody looks at the emperor's clothes and marvels at it. Well, that is what we do. The ego made up this world to be a distraction device and we marvel at it, and say what a wonderful world this is. What an incredible cosmos this is. Let's study it, and let's study how the world began. Or let's study this marvelous creation called the body. And let's study everything about the body. Or the marvelous thing called the psyche. And let's try to study the psyche.

The whole thing is made up; there is nothing here. The emperor has no clothes on. That is the judgment that the Holy Spirit makes. And that is the only thing that is understandable about the ego, is that it is nothing. That is understandable. It is understandable that everything I think I think, everything I think I feel, everything I think I do, is all made up.

It is all an attempt to distract me from what my ego has first made real; namely, that I am separate from God. All the judgments we make based upon form are all nothing because the form is nothing. There is literally nothing here. Once again, that is why the Holy Spirit doesn't do anything in the world. That kind of thought can work well with other spiritual systems, but it is not what *A Course in Miracles* teaches.

The Holy Spirit's judgment is not anything outside. His judgment is, there is nothing outside. You are upset because you think there is something there, but there is nothing there. You are upset because you believe you made up a world that can take the place of Heaven. You believe you made up a self that can take the place of Christ. You believe you made up an emotion that you call love that can take the place of real love. That is the judgment, and that is what form is. So again:

(T-14.X.8:8-9) Yet they but study form with meaningless content. For their teacher is senseless, though careful to conceal this fact behind impressive sounding words, but which lack any consistent sense when they are put together.

If we really look at everything the ego thought system teaches us in all its myriad forms in our world, and we really try to understand it, we'd realize it makes no sense, because it teaches the opposite of God. It teaches that separation is real, differentiation is real, judgment is real and justified, that we can make judgments that are true, that the world is real, etc., etc. That love is getting and stealing and bargaining and compromising, that love is sacrifice, that love is death, etc., etc.

If we really look at all of this and put the whole package together, we'd realize it makes no sense. But it only makes no sense when we lift ourselves above the battleground and look back down on it, and say it makes no sense. Within the battleground, it makes perfect sense to study the body, because that is what I believe I am. It makes perfect sense to study all the diseases and sicknesses in the world, because that is what I believe happens to me when I get sick and there is something wrong with me. It makes no sense when you lift yourself above the battleground and you look down on the body and say, it is not a disease. It is not a bacteria that makes me sick. It is guilt that makes me sick.

All the other things that go on, all the impressive sounding words that the ego puts forth, whether it talks about medicine or psychology or astrology or astronomy or physics or biology or chemistry, make no sense when you lift yourself above the body. It makes perfect sense if you believe you are a body, that you study yourself. But all that we are doing is studying the ego, which is exactly what the ego wants.

Cannibalism is the Motto of the Ego

Q: Obviously, the ego is not going to tell us all this, especially that what we're trying to do is kill everyone. What is it that the ego does tell us?

A: The ego simply is trying to tell us that the way you'll avoid the awful pain that you are in, because there is something so wrong with you and you are such a miserable, creepy worm—the way you avoid that is to join with other people, steal their strength and put it on yourself, and then you'll feel better about yourself.

Q: That's what cannibalism is?

A: Yes. Cannibalism is the motto of the ego. The way that the ego came into being within its own thought system is to cannibalize God. It stole from God. That is why the whole world is a cannibalistic one. That is what the body is. There is no way a body can live without food. Well, what is food? Food is another body. Whether you are talking about an animal or you are talking about a plant, it doesn't make any difference. The only way we can survive is to steal or take something from outside and put it within.

In order to survive we have to have oxygen. The only way to do this is to breathe, which means we have to take oxygen from outside and put it inside and cannibalize it. Now we don't usually think about it as cannibalism, because we think about, that is what bodies do. In order for a body to survive, it has to breathe oxygen. In order for a body to survive, it has to eat food. Well, that is true within the body's law.

But what you are really doing is killing something outside. And then we say, well, some things it is okay if I kill and other things it is not okay if I kill. It is okay if I kill a carrot and eat it, but it is not okay if I kill an animal and eat it. If there is a difference between a carrot and an animal, there is a difference in form. The content is the same. The content is, neither of them is alive.

The ego always makes judgments. It is okay if I eat certain foods, but not other foods, based upon the idea that some things are more alive than others, or some things are holier than others. But that is the ego's judgment. The Holy Spirit's judgment is that they are all unreal. One is no more alive than another. And therefore, what difference does it make?

Meditation

The session begins with Ken introducing a poem which he will use as a meditation. "The Quiet Dream" from *The Gifts of God*, page 65.

This is a poem about forgiveness and forgiveness as the means whereby we attain the quiet dream, which is a another way of speaking about what the Course calls the happy dream or the real world, which is a way of looking at this world without judgment, which obviously is the theme of the workshop. To see a world with no condemnation and no sin in it.

The Quiet Dream

Help me forgive the world, my Lord. For then
The quiet comes in which the dream is done.
The wanderer comes home, the lame arise,
The sightless see. For fear cannot approach
The wholly sinless world forgiveness sees.
Let its soft light awaken sight in me,
And seeing, let the dream of fear be gone.

I have no choice but to forgive the world.
The dream that peace can come another way
Is sick illusion. Christ accepts a dream
His Father shines upon. Behold this dream;
It is His gift to me. Look on a world
So gentle and so still no leaf can fall,
And not one blade of grass can be destroyed.

There is a light that shines upon this world,
And judges it as Christ would have it judged.
There is no condemnation on it. He
Beholds it sinless, in the light that shines
From His Own face. His vision looks upon
The sure reflection of His Father's Love;
The picture calling up His memory.

What can remain of evil in the world
Christ's vision looks upon? And what could still
Appear to me as fearful, with the light
Of His perfection on it? What could teach
Me sorrow has a cause, or death is real?
Help me forgive the world. The peace You give
In my forgiveness will be given me.

The Equality of Miracles (cont.)

Let's turn back to the text, page 295 where we left off yesterday afternoon. We stopped at the second paragraph on that page. What we ended up with in the preceding paragraph is the idea how the ego always urges us to study itself, and study all of its miscreations, both the physical universe and then all the theories and thoughts that we have of the body, the psyche, etc. Obviously, all this does is make the error real, make the body real, make the world real, make the psyche real, and we just go around and around and around.

We can never really understand any of these things, because we have forgotten where they came from. When the world, when the scientists, when the philosophers and psychologists and theologians, etc., etc., all try to study some aspect of this physical world, whether again we are talking about the cosmos or the world or the body, or the psyche or theology of whatever form it is—we are only studying it within itself, as if it were independent and separate from the mind. We can never understand it, because again we have forgotten that all of this is caused by the belief in sin, which in itself is nonexistent.

All that we are doing is literally studying and trying to understand and explain something that is not there. When you look at it that way, obviously the fruitlessness of it all becomes very apparent. But that is the whole idea. The ego never lets us look at the fact that this is futile. Instead we think that there really is something to be gained by studying the different aspects of the world, seeking to understand, control, explain, predict, etc.

So we will pick up again on the second paragraph on that page.

(T-14.X.9:1-2) This is characteristic of the ego's judgments. Separately, they seem to hold...

If I believe my body is real and then I study an aspect of my body, that makes sense. Or if I believe that the physical world is real and I study some aspects or some laws of the physical world like the law of gravity, etc., then that makes sense. But when I put the whole package together, as it will say in just a minute, then I realize it makes no sense because it is all based upon form, it is all based upon difference, it is all based upon judgment. And above all, it is based upon the idea that I know what is really going on, and that I am the one who can really understand and make a reasonable judgment.

(T-14.X.9:2-3) Separately, they seem to hold, but put them together and the system of thought that arises from joining them is incoherent and utterly chaotic. [Because again, what we are doing is making the illusion real, and saying there is a reality outside of Heaven.] **For form is not enough for meaning, and the underlying lack of content makes a cohesive system impossible.**

Now when the Course says a "lack of content" what it is really talking about is a lack of love or a lack of truth, because obviously the ego does have a content, which is guilt, which underlies everything. Here when Jesus speaks of a lack of content, what he's talking about is a lack of true content. Else-where, the Course talks about the two emotions that we have, love and fear, and it says one we made and one was given us (T-13.V.10:1). The emotion which was given us, of course, is love; and the emotion that we made is fear.

Basically, emotion really is not quite the correct word—*thought* would be better—because it is really thought that underlies emotion. There are just but two thoughts or two emotions or two contents—love and fear, truth and illusion, God and the ego. And of these, only one is true. So again, when Jesus says the underlying lack of content, he really means the underlying lack of true content. There is no love in anything in this world, there is no truth in anything in this world. When we look at things in the world, then we realize not only how complicated they are but how contradictory things are.

(T-14.X.9:4-7) Separation therefore remains the ego's chosen condition. [That *is* what the content is.] **For no one alone can judge the ego truly. Yet when two or more join together in searching for truth, the ego can no longer defend its lack of content. The fact of union tells them it is not true.**

The underlying content of the ego, the underlying thought that underlies everything in this world and all of our thoughts about this world is the thought of separation or the thought of difference or the thought of judgment. Because, once again, that is the original thought that gave rise to the ego in the first place. It is the "fact" that the Son of God can be separate from his Creator. And because that is the original thought, and all split minds and all fragmentary minds came from that thought, we all share that same basic content.

When I try to understand the ego and I believe that I am a body understanding something that is outside of me, there is no way that I can understand it. Because the very fact that I believe I am doing this with my brain and my body, and studying something that is separate from me, is reinforcing the very lack of content, the very lack of truth or the very illusion that is present; except I am not aware of that.

So it is basically the ego studying itself. We have nothing studying nothing, and the end result, of course, is nothing. But the ego tells us that it is something and that we can judge the difference between the various somethings here without, again, realizing that it is all nothing. When we join together— and this statement, of course, is taken from the famous gospel statement where Jesus says, "Where two or three are gathered in my name, there am I in their midst." When we really join with another person, which means that we no longer see the other person's interests as separate from our own, then that is the undoing of the belief in separation.

When I no longer see you as different from me, then I look beyond the form and I disregard the differences in form. The difference is that you are out there and I am here, so I think, and you are of one sex and I am another. You believe one thing, I believe another, etc. I disregard all those superficial differences and I rather experience the oneness that we both share, not only the oneness in Christ that we share, which is beyond our recognition at this point, but the oneness of the ego thought system that we share.

We all share the same hope and yearning to return home. That is what joins us. When I make that the reality, then I am no longer concerned with studying something that is of form. Because I have now made the content what is important. By disregarding the form in you and the form in me, and realizing that makes no difference and that is superficial, I am teaching myself that form is nothing and content is everything. And the content that is everything is the joining and the unity of you and me as we are two brothers or sisters walking down the same journey, the same pathway home, which is the reminder and the reflection that not only are you and I one, but Christ and God are one as well.

(T-14.X.10:1-3) It is impossible to remember God in secret and alone. For remembering Him means you are not alone, and are willing to remember it. Take no thought for yourself, for no thought you hold *is* for yourself.

This is just another way of saying the same idea. Right at the beginning, once again, what gave the ego its birth and what gave it its continuing existence within the dream is the belief that we indeed are separate from God. That is the original belief in differences and the original judgment. We are separate from God and we have an existence as independent and outside of God's Mind.

Since that is the original ego thought, which is the foundation for the split mind, and each of us is a fragment of that split mind, we all share that same basic belief that this is what will save us. Right at the beginning, the separated Son of God believes that what keeps his existence intact is insuring that he is separate from God. To keep that barrier between himself and God rigid and firm and clear, he then makes up a world and a body that then establishes a barrier between himself and God. Remember the line I quoted earlier in the workshop that this world was made as an attack on God and was made to be a place where God could enter not (W-pII.3.2:1). There is now a barrier or a fortress, which is an even better word, between ourselves and God.

The body, then, also becomes a barrier, not only between ourselves and God but between ourselves and everyone else, which must be the case as long as we hold to the basic ego premise that we are separate. Since that is the basic problem, the undoing of that problem, which is really what the meaning of forgiveness is, is to recognize that despite the seeming barriers between ourselves, which are the bodies that you seem to inhabit and I seem to inhabit—that despite those barriers, we are still joined sharing the same purpose. There is a line right at the beginning of the teacher's manual, on page 3, at the top of the page, and it says:

(M-1.1:1-2) A teacher of God is anyone who chooses to be one. His qualifications consist solely in this; somehow, somewhere he has made a deliberate choice in which he did not see his interests as apart from someone else's.

Another way of saying this in the context of this workshop is that that is the moment when we no longer judge somebody else. Judging always excludes. I am the one who's judging you. And that is separating. There is no love in that. It is not done with a desire to help. It is done with a desire to exclude and separate.

What establishes us as a teacher of God, and of course, that is what we are all aspiring to be in terms of being students of the Course, is to recognize that no one's interest is separate from our own. The ego's plan for salvation, of course, is to see that our interests are separate and my interests are best served at your expense. The way that I escape from the horror of my own guilt and from the terrible burden of my self-hatred (which is my only need) is to take it from myself and project it onto you and attack you and accuse you, and make you responsible for all the misery that I am feeling. My salvation then rests on your being attacked. I become the victim and you become the victimizer. I become the sinless and you become the sinner.

Clearly at this point, our interests are separate. Because I don't care about you; I just care about me. Judgment, then, is another way of talking about how that dynamic works. As long as I do that, I cannot remember God, because I have excluded God by excluding you. That is the way that the Course integrates its metaphysical teachings on the illusory nature of this world and of the purity and the unity of God with our experience in this world. The way that I remember God and awaken from this awful, awful dream is to simply join with another person.

That is what forgiveness is all about. That is why forgiveness is the Course's central teaching. I don't have to actually experience my unity with God. I don't have to experience that original moment of terror when I believe I separated from Him and made that judgment. All that I have to do is simply join with one other person totally. And obviously, it is the totally that makes forgiveness into a process, because it is not something that we do all that quickly. Because if I could truly join with you, I am undoing the very belief in separation which upholds the entire thought system of the ego. Just as, by attacking you and judging you and criticizing you and excluding you, I am upholding the entire thought system of the ego, and reinforcing it.

Joining

Q: How do you join with another person?

A: That's a good question. When the Course talks about joining with another person, which again is what the end of judgment is and the end of the ego is, it does not literally mean that you join with someone else. Because if I have to join with you, what I am doing is making real the fact that I am not joined with you. That is why, when the Course talks about what the miracle is, and when it talks about what forgiveness is, and it talks about what salvation is, it never talks about what they do.

It always describes them as undoing. The miracle doesn't do; it undoes. Forgiveness doesn't do; it undoes. It talks about how the miracle simply looks on devastation. It just "looks on devastation and reminds the mind that what it sees is false" (W-pII.13.1.3). When the Course talks about joining, even though the words seem to suggest that you have to join with someone, what it is really talking about is undoing the belief in separation that conceals from us the fact that we are already joined.

In other words, I don't have to join with you because I am already one with you. The separation has had no effect on the basic unity of Christ. You and I are already one. The problem is, I've covered over that experience of unity with layers and layers and layers of judgment, separation, projections, attack thoughts, etc. Which means all I have to do is undo them, like you peel layers off an onion. I undo the thoughts of attack and the thoughts of difference and the thoughts of judgment. When those are undone, what is left is my awareness and experience of the unity and the joining that was always there. So basically, joining is simply undoing.

What makes living in the real world so easy and everything else so difficult is that when you are in the real world, you literally do nothing. Because you realize there is nothing that has to be done. You simply are done through, in the sense that it is the love of the Holy Spirit that comes through us, and we don't do anything. It doesn't mean, as I mentioned earlier, that our bodies don't do things. But I no longer experience my self, my ego self, as the agent or the doer of what my body is doing.

It is the love of God that comes through me, and that is what does. All that I have to do is, as the workbook says, step back and let Him lead the way (W-pI.155). The stepping back is a stepping back from the ego. Forgiveness or the miracle are the means by which that happens. Joining is simply undoing the barriers of separation. I don't have to join with you. I just have to be aware of my separating thoughts towards you; my anger towards you, my special love needs, my special hate needs. That is what I have to become aware of.

As I become aware of them and say to Jesus, "Oh, I am doing it again. I really believe by excluding Katie and by using Katie in this way, I am keeping your love away from me." That's silly. But obviously I am still afraid of your love, so I am using Katie as the means whereby I can keep you away. And just looking at that in that way is what joining is.

Q: Are you saying that theoretically, I can join with someone whose views are completely different from mine and who has completely different ways of doing things?

A: Right. You don't deny that there are differences. You don't deny that there are differences of opinion with someone. You simply deny that the differences of opinion make a difference—excuse the pun. You know, sometimes people say, how can I stay with this partner I am with? How can I stay married to this person or living with this person? He or she is not a student of the Course. If I stay with this person, it will impede my progress, etc. Well, very often that is the perfect person for you to stay with, because it is a wonderful way of learning the lesson that the differences of opinion, the differences in spiritual paths don't count for anything.

Q: So I can do this even with someone who doesn't want to join with me. For example, in the typical adversarial business situation. I can do this all by myself?

A: Yes. You can only do it by yourself because there is no one else. There is no one outside you. There is no adversary outside of you. There is an adversary within you, which is yourself. One way of understanding this, which I think is helpful, is that you can be in a relationship with someone which obviously is unhealed. And then that person dies. Does that mean that you can nevermore be forgiven or forgive because the person is no longer there? Obviously, it doesn't mean that.

You could still work on forgiving a relationship even if the person died 30 years ago. Because relationships are in the mind, for the simple reason that there is nothing else but the mind. What we do is we take the relationships in our mind, and ultimately everything is a projection of our relationship with God, and we project that onto a body. The illusion is, I forgive this body that is there. In reality, all I am doing is withdrawing the projections of guilt from my own mind that I placed onto that body.

It doesn't make a difference if the other person is physically present, is physically alive, or if the other person is aware of what you are doing or even cares what you are doing. Or maybe the person is opposing what you are doing. Forgiveness is still possible. At the moment that you forgive that person, that person is also forgiven, even if he or she has not accepted it as yet. There is a line in the Course that says how the Holy Spirit saves all of those forgiving thoughts until the person is ready to accept them.

There is another line in a very beautiful passage, where Jesus says, I have saved all your loving thoughts and kindnesses (T.5.IV.8:3). Basically, he saves them until the time we can accept them for ourselves. You don't need the other person's conscious approval or willingness or even physical presence in order to forgive. Relationships are the home of the Holy Spirit, as the Course explains, but again, relationships are not external; they are in our minds. We forgive in the context of what appears to be a relationship with a body outside of us because that is the illusion; that is the dream. That is why the Course explains that forgiveness is also an illusion, because it forgives what never was. It also forgives who never was, because there was never anybody there.

The Equality of Miracles (cont.)

Let's go back to 295. We're in the third paragraph, fourth line.

(T-14.X.10:4) If you would remember your Father, [which of course is what the goal of the Course is. Actually, it is not the goal. It is what comes after. The goal, which amounts to a formula in the Course, is that you see the face of Christ in your brother (which is what forgiveness and the purpose of the Course is) and then you remember God. If you would remember your Father,] **let the Holy Spirit order your thoughts and give only the answer with which He answers you.**

What this is talking about really is the same issue that we had discussed yesterday. All of our thoughts are disordered, because our thoughts all come from the basic thought of the ego that we are separate from God, which obviously is a disordered thought. It is a thought that is chaotic, because it disregards and disrupts what order is.

The true Order—we spell with a capital "O"—is God and Christ are perfectly unified. That is the true Order of thought. When we "separate" from God, we rupture that unity and that is what makes that thought disordered, and all the subsequent thoughts disordered. The only Ordered thought in our mind is that memory of God's Love, that memory of the unity of Heaven, and that is what the Holy Spirit is. If I want to truly remember God, which everyone would claim—whether one actually believes in God or not, everyone wants to return home. Everyone wants to have that experience of love and safety that is a dim, dim memory in our mind.

What Jesus is saying to us is that if we are truly serious about that and truly want to go back home and want to experience love, then the way to do that is to turn over to the Holy Spirit our investment in maintaining that we are right, that the separation from God is true, and that our judgments against God and against ourselves and against each other, are valid. What we are asked to do then is to turn over all of our disordered thoughts, our thoughts of judgment, our thoughts of attack, our thoughts of guilt, etc., etc., to the Holy Spirit, and then let Him order them for us.

As we saw yesterday, the way that He orders our thoughts or corrects our thoughts is to have us realize that all of our thoughts have to do with things that are external to us. All of our thoughts have to do with attack and judgment. All of our thoughts have to do with the consequences of sin that we perceive outside of us. The way the Holy Spirit heals all of those thoughts is to bring them back to their source, which is our decision in our mind to be an ego, the decision in our mind to make sin and separation real. When we go back to that cause, we can then judge that cause with Him and then we smile at it. We realize that all of my other thoughts and all of my other feelings and beliefs are coming from a fear of getting back to that place of love in our mind, and looking at that cause and smiling at it.

(T-14.X.10:5) Everyone seeks for love as you do, [And this obviously should be taken very literally. Everyone seeks for love. The world's greatest sinners, the Adolf Hitler's and everyone else, all the cruel and malicious rapists in the world and the thieves in the world and the murderers in the world, are all calling out for love, just as we are.] **but knows it not unless he joins with you in seeking it.**

The only way that we will remember the love that we are seeking is to join with another person. If you have done something terrible, either to hurt me or somebody whom I identify with, and I make that judgment, that you have done something terrible, what I am doing is I am telling you that you are right. What I am telling you is that judgment is correct, attack is correct, separation is correct and differences are correct. Because I am doing the very same thing you are doing, or the very same thing that I am accusing you of doing.

The ego in my mind is reinforcing the ego in your mind. Even though I am trying to say that you and I are different. That you have done a terrible thing and I know that. That you are the victimizer and I am the victim. And even though on the level of form, I seem to be coming at you from a totally different point of view, it is really the exact same content. I am making attack real and judgment real and separation real. Thereby, I am telling you, you are right, which reinforces your belief in your ego and obviously does the same thing for myself.

What the Course is always trying to help us do is to recognize that what our task is, is to tell our brother that his sin against us has had no effect. Which means that no matter what you have done to me or to somebody else, the love and the peace of God within my mind has not changed. When I am angry at you and I judge against you, I am telling you your sin has had an effect. My anger is the witness to what you have done.

Or it can take another form. You are someone whom I care about and you are upset, and I feel badly for you, and I feel sorry for you. I am doing the very same thing. I am making your error real. I am saying yes, you should be upset. This is a harsh, cruel world, where people abandon you, where people take advantage of you, where people victimize you and they do this, that and the other thing to you, and you are absolutely right.

Once again, it seems as if I am loving you and I am joining with you. In reality, all that I am doing is reinforcing your thought system of separation as well as doing the same thing for myself. Again, I am not talking about behavior. I am not talking about saying comforting words to someone who is upset. I am talking about the part of your mind that gets upset and feels indeed, that yes, you are perfectly justified in being hurt, angry, sad, etc. The only way that I can truly help you is to be the reminder for you of the truth that is in both of our minds.

We discussed yesterday how Jesus is a manifestation of the Holy Spirit, and we are asked by the Course to be his manifestation in the world. But all that we are asked to do is to be this reminder for each other of that healing truth that is inside of all of us, which is a truth in which there is no judgment. It is a truth which looks on the cause of all suffering and pain and smiles at it.

If you are very upset and I become upset with you and for you, I am saying, "Yes, this is an awful world and we should be upset." In other words, that these are heavy consequences that are here, and they are split off from their cause. When I am able not to be upset or not to be angry with you, whether I am upset for you or upset against you, what I am saying is that what has caused your pain, which is the belief in separation, has no power. Sin has no effect; and therefore, it is not a cause. What I am really showing you is how to smile at the ego's cause, and then it disappears.

(T-14.X.10:6-7) If you undertake the search together, [this is the search for love] you bring with you a light so powerful that what you see is given meaning. The lonely journey fails because it has excluded what it would find.

The lonely journey is that I make it by myself. Again, we are not talking about behavior. This does not mean that your partner has to agree with you. This doesn't mean that your partner has to be *A Course in Miracles'* student who is doing the daily workbook lessons with you. What it means is that in my mind, I do not seek Heaven by myself. I do not believe that I could find the peace and the love of God and what would make me happy, at your expense. That is what this is talking about.

When the Course says no one enters Heaven by himself, or the ark of peace is entered two by two (T-20.IV.6:5), or salvation is a collaborative venture (T-4.VI.8:2), or statements such as here, it does not mean that you literally have to do it with another person who is doing it with you. Because if that were so, then that would make you dependent on somebody else. And would mean if someone else doesn't do it with you, then you now are the victim of that other person's reluctance to be a holy, spiritual person like yourself. That obviously goes against everything that the Course is saying. What it is talking about is that, in my mind, I realize that I cannot get to Heaven and harbor attack thoughts against you or anyone else. That is what this means.

Q: Ken, how do you relate that to the idea that you can never be healed alone?

A: Well, it's the same thing. In other words, my ego tells me that all of my problems can be solved and healed by myself. I can do it by myself. I don't need you. And that you are the cause of my problems. The healing then, is to get rid of you. That is obvious and that is clear from the ego's point of view.

When it says, "When I am healed I am not healed alone" (W-pI.137) it both means that I can only be healed through an act of joining in my mind. It also is telling me that all minds are joined. When I am healed, when I accept the Atonement for myself and I identify with that love of God within me, then since minds are joined and we are all thoughts in the same mind, then everyone is healed the same way.

That is the same idea as when Jesus says, "You were with me when I arose." What he means is not obviously that we were physically with him. It doesn't mean that we are all healed of our dream just because he is. What it does mean is he is a thought in the mind of the Sonship just as we all are. And thoughts are joined. He then becomes an expression in form of that light of the Atonement, or the light of the resurrection. We were with him when he arose, because we are always with him. We still have to accept what he has accepted.

Q: So joining with another person does not mean that they have to believe the same thing you believe?

A: It has nothing to do with form. *It has nothing to do with form*, and thought is form. You could have a very happy relationship with someone who doesn't believe in any of this; who not only is not a student of the Course but is not interested in any spirituality in form. You can have a very fulfilled and happy and loving and forgiving relationship. It has nothing whatsoever to do with form. People think, "Wouldn't it be lovely if I could find someone, or my partner shared this with me." Well, on the level of form, yes, it would seem nice.

But remember again, we don't know what our best interests are. There is an early workbook lesson, "I do not perceive my own best interests" (W-pI.24). It might just be that my learning path will be accelerated and my learning will be strengthened being with someone who doesn't share this on the level of form. Because that is how I learn that differences don't matter. The differences in form don't matter, and that we are all the same.

Q: It seems like yesterday, with judgment, every past judgment in my life has been bombarding me as I've been sitting here for two days.

A: Aren't you glad you came? (laughter) If you could let your mind be bombarded by all those judgments, and step back and look at it with the Holy Spirit next to you, then you are no longer doing it alone and the judgments won't seem quite as awful. And after awhile, you'll smile at them and say, "Yeah, of course that is going to happen." My ego's in outrage. And it should be in outrage.

Then what you do is you now have a tool that you can use to help you deal with them. The tool in the past was to deny them and repress them. That is the magical, ostrich-like hope that if I don't see the problem, it is not there. That is a tool we are all very good at. We deny that all the time. What happens now is that you realize there is a better way of dealing with my problems. I don't have to run away from them, I don't have to deny them, I don't have to be ashamed of them or guilty about them or afraid of them. I can look at them. And I can look at them with the love of Jesus or the Holy Spirit with me. I look at them and learn how to smile at them. Then they stop being problems. Then they become learning opportunities.

Let's skip to the top of page 295 the second line.

(T-14.X.11:4) Every interpretation you would lay upon a brother is senseless.

This is another way of saying that every judgment that we make against, or put upon another person, is senseless because it is from the ego. It is seeing you as different from me and that is what enables me to make a judgment against you. It certainly gives me the idea that I have the wisdom to know what you are, what you should be, what is best for you, what is best for me, what is best for others. All the judgments that we make, make no sense because they are all coming from the ego, which makes no sense, because the ego begins with a premise that makes no sense; namely, that we can indeed be separate from God. From that senseless thought arises a senseless thought system, a senseless world, and then the senselessness that all of us share.

(T-14.X.11:5-6) Let the Holy Spirit show him to you, [In other words, let us ask the Holy Spirit to look at this person with us] **and teach you both his love and his call for love.** [Well that is that same idea that we have been talking about] **Neither his mind nor yours holds more than these two orders of thought.**

The Course explains in many other places besides here that there is no other alternative or option in this world. We either choose the ego or the Holy Spirit, and there is no other choice. We must choose one of the two, but there is no other choice. When we choose the Holy Spirit, then He has us recognize that anything someone does is either an expression of love or a call for love. An expression of love obviously comes when that person identifies with the Holy Spirit. When that person identifies with the ego, which is the other option, then that is not something that is hateful, that is evil, that is sinful; rather, it is something that comes from fear, and fear is simply a call for the love that has been denied.

Basically, on a very practical level what we do, and this really is what the meaning of forgiveness is, when we find ourselves holding attack thoughts towards someone else or judgmental thoughts or critical thoughts or angry thoughts— whatever the form—then we would realize this must be coming from my ego. I am choosing to be upset and to be angry and to hold judgments because I am afraid of the love that is really in my mind. And the way to exclude that love is to exclude somebody else.

At that point, I realize what I am doing and I stop. That is all I have to do. Just realize what I am doing. Simply looking at my ego and realizing why it is I am choosing it is enough of an invitation to the Holy Spirit to let His light begin to shine through me. But all my part is, is simply to look at what I am doing and give that to Him. And giving it to Him simply means looking at it with Him.

It doesn't mean handing it over to Him or saying some kind of formula or mantra. What it means is an actual process within our minds whereby we look at our angry thoughts, our ego thoughts, and say yes, that is what I am doing. I am never upset for the reason I think (W-pI.5). I am choosing to be upset because I am afraid of God's Love and God's peace. And I am just using this as an excuse, which camouflages the decision I have made. It is a way of denying the responsibility that I have for how I feel.

There is a series of statements on page 448 in the text, that begins: "I am responsible for what I see" (T-21.II.2:3). What it is talking about is that I am responsible for the way that I am seeing it. You are not responsible for my being angry no matter what you have done. I am responsible for my being angry, because I have chosen to be angry because I believe being angry or being anxious or being sick or being fearful is better for me than the love of God. That is all I have to do. Our job is to bring that illusion to His light and to His truth.

How Can Perception of Order of Difficulties be Avoided?

Let's turn to the teacher's manual. We will begin on page 24. There are two sections in the manual that deal specifically with judgment. This one that is called, "How can perception of order of difficulties be avoided?" and then on page 27, "How is judgment relinquished?" We will start with the second paragraph.

(M-8.2:1-2) Illusions are always illusions of differences. How could it be otherwise?

We have already seen that the entire thought system of the ego, which is illusory, is based upon the original judgment and perception of difference.

(M-8.2:3) By definition, an illusion is an attempt to make something real that is regarded as of major impor- tance, but is recognized as being untrue.

That is what we do. The ego thought system is basically untrue. It is a falsity. And yet that is what we try to make real.

(M-8.2:4) The mind therefore seeks to make it true out of its intensity of desire to have it for itself.

What the ego wants to do is sustain its own existence and take its inherently illusory being and nonexistence and make it into something that seems to have reality. What is important about that statement is the phrase "intensity of desire." In other words, it is something that I choose. The reason I make your sins real is because I want you to be sinful. Not because you are sinful; not because of anything that you've done. I want you to be sinful. Therefore, in my mind, you have become sinful.

(M-8.2:5-6) Illusions are travesties of creation; [Just as I mentioned the other day, the body is talked about earlier as being a travesty of creation. Illusions are travesties of creation.] **attempts to bring truth to lies.** [Rather again, what we are asked to do is to bring the lie to the truth.] **Finding truth unacceptable** [This is from the ego's point of view. Once our decision maker has identified with the ego thought system, truth now has become unacceptable, because truth means the undoing of the ego. Truth is the Atonement prin- ciple that the separation never happened. So, finding truth unacceptable] **the mind revolts against truth and gives itself an illusion of victory.**

That is exactly what the ego has done. It finds the truth of God's Love and God's creation unacceptable because it means the end of the ego. Therefore, the ego fights against truth, sets up a battleground in which it makes God or truth into the enemy. Then it believes that it has become victorious over God. The way that we believe that we become victorious over

God is that we really believe we are here. If we are here, then God must be a lie. Because God is pure spirit, and creation is only of Him and is only of spirit.

Well, if I am here in a body and there is this whole cosmos of form that changes, decomposes and dies—all of which is the exact opposite of Heaven—then that means I have triumphed over God. The Course explains in special relationships, every one, every specialness that we are involved with is an attempt to triumph over God (T-16.V.10:1). The good feeling that we get when someone else does what we want is really coming because it is the reminder of the ego, "See, I told you. We have triumphed over God and we have done it again." We have stolen from somebody else what that person has withheld from us. It has now become our own. We have once again triumphed and we are the people who are on the throne of creation. We are God. That is the ecstasy, that is the passion, that is the power. That is the seeming joy of specialness. We have once again triumphed and we have proven that we can have what we want and we can get it.

(M-8.2:7) Finding health a burden, it retreats into feverish dreams.

The health it is talking about is the health of the Holy Spirit —true healing. Since that is the problem, from the ego's point of view, it retreats into its illusions of health, which obviously is sickness and pain.

(M-8.2:8) And in these dreams [which would really be all the dreams of the world] **the mind is separate, different from other minds, with different interests of its own, and able to gratify its needs at the expense of others.**

You probably couldn't get a more succinct and powerful statement of what the whole motivation of the ego world is. And what it is. In other words, in these dreams, which is everything in this world and all of our experiences in this world, minds are separate, they are different from everyone else, because we believe we are all different. Our interests are different. And above all, I can have my needs met at your expense.

And of course, that is what all special relationships are about. I need something. You won't give it to me so I am going to get it from you. I am either going to get it from you by a direct attack, which is what the Course refers to as special hate. Or I get it from you from an indirect attack, which we call special love, which is whereby I seduce you into giving me what you don't really want to give me. I make the insane bargains that we always make with each other.

But the idea is that I have a need within me that God cannot meet, but you can meet it. The you can be another person, it can be a drug, it can be alcohol, it can be another body, it could be money, it could be fame, it could be anything of the world. But what I am saying is, God can't meet my need, but this other thing can. If this other thing can, and I take it from you, you don't have it and I have it. That is the idea of having needs gratified at the expense of somebody else. The only need that we have, as the Course explains, is to forgive. Because in forgiveness, we recognize that we have no needs. Forgiveness undoes the belief that there are needs that God cannot fulfill, but other people can.

(M-8.4:1-2) It is in the sorting out and categorizing activities of the mind that errors in perception enter. And it is here correction must be made.

If we look at perception just as a phenomenon of the body, it cannot exist without judgment. As I mentioned right at the beginning Friday evening, it is impossible in this world, within the dream, to avoid judgment. It is impossible to perceive without judgment. You cannot perceive without some recognition or some expression of figure and ground, which is a perceptual term. Ground is the background or the context, and the figures are what you choose to focus on.

Everyone makes judgments. A clear example of that would be, if I walk into this room and I am an interior decorator, I am not interested in all the people here. The people here will simply fade into the background and will become the ground. The figure, or what I am focusing on, would be the different colors and the color scheme and the arrangement of the furniture and the curtains, etc., etc. That is what I will focus on.

If I am interested in lighting and I am a lighting expert, and I am interested in how the light works in this room, I am not going to be interested in the colors. I am not going to be interested in what is outside. I am not going to be interested in the people. I will be interested in the light. Lighting will become the figure and everything else will become the ground. And I make the judgment that all that is important for me now is to study the lighting in the room.

If I am giving a workshop, then my focus is not on the lighting; my focus is not on what is outside. It is not on the arrangement of the chairs. It is focusing on the people. The people become what is important and I make a judgment, that is what I am focusing on. That becomes the figure and the ground becomes the rest of the room.

Now there is nothing wrong about that. We all have to do that. Otherwise, we couldn't exist, obviously. We have learned at a very early age, so it becomes automatic, how to filter out stimuli that are not essential to us. Other times when we have made tape recordings, I'll be speaking, and I don't hear external noises. But then if I play back the tape, I hear birds, I hear cars going by, etc., which I don't hear while I am talking because that is not what is important.

On this level, it is impossible to avoid judgment and the Course is not saying that we shouldn't judge on that level. What it is talking about are the judgments we make whose purposes are of the ego; namely, the purposes are to attack. Then, I declare as nonessential all the good things about you. All that I am interested in is finding some flaw, something that you have said wrong, something you have done wrong, something you have thought wrong. That is what I focus on. And that becomes the figure and everything else becomes the background.

Forgiveness then would be a term that we give to the process of learning to reverse the figure and the ground. Rather than focus on all the negative things that you do, rather what I focus on is the positive things you do. And even more to the point, what it means is I reinterpret all of what my ego would call something negative in you, something sinful in you; I reinterpret it and I call it, "a call for help." Because if I see what you are doing as a sin, I am saying that you are different and separate from me. If I am seeing what you are doing as a call for love, then I am seeing what you are doing is a call for love and what I am doing is a call for love. So we are both united. And that becomes what I focus on. That, then, is a positive use of judgment. It is a judgment whose purpose is not to exclude or to attack, but rather to join.

Page 24, the third paragraph, I'll reread those first two lines.

(M-8.4:1-2) It is in the sorting out and categorizing activities of the mind that errors in perception enter. And it is here correction must be made.

Now what is particularly important here, obviously, is that the correction must be made on the level of the mind. The problem is not what my body's eyes see. The problem is not my body's eyes. The problem is my mind. For example, if something happens to my physical eyes, I then go to an eye doctor who takes care of my eyes and then I believe I can see again.

What it doesn't take care of is the decision that my mind made to attack my eyes, and attack my vision. That is not touched at all. All that has happened is that the symptom has been taken care of. The effect has been changed. But the cause of the blindness or the impaired vision has not been dealt with. That is what this is saying. The correction must be made on the level of the mind. Now this doesn't mean, again, that you don't see an ophthalmologist. It simply means that don't believe that having your eyes checked and fixed on the level of the body is going to correct the cause of the blindness or the impaired vision.

(M-8.4:3) The mind classifies what the body's eyes bring to it according to its preconceived values, [and the "its" refers to the mind] **judging where each sense datum fits best.**

Again, this is the idea that we have already talked about in relationship to lesson 151. It is the mind that makes the judgments. Using the example I used a moment ago right before the break, when I walk into this room, there is a judgment that is made. It is that I will pay attention to the people in the room and not to the décor. But it is not my eyes that make that judgment. It is not my brain that makes that judgment. It is my mind that makes that judgment. And because it is my mind which is a disordered mind that has a foundation with a disordered thought—the thought being guilt—then everything that I perceive and I value and I judge will be wrong.

(M-8.4:4-5) What basis could be faultier than this? Unrecognized by itself, it has itself asked to be given what will fit into these categories.

So again, it is the mind that makes the choice, sends out a messenger to bring back those messages that it wants. Basically, there are only two kinds of messages that can be brought back—one is the ego's message, and the other is the Holy Spirit's message. One is the message of judgment, conflict, separation, suffering, pain and death. The other is the message of forgiveness, unity, love and forgiveness.

(M-8.4:6-8) And having done so, it concludes that the categories must be true. On this the judgment of all differences rests, because it is on this that judgments of the world

depend. Can this confused and senseless "reasoning" be depended on for anything?

When it is spoken about in this way, obviously, the answer is no. But none of us looks at it this way. None of us really stops to think that maybe everything that I am perceiving and thinking and judging is wrong. We don't think it is wrong because our bodies tell us that it is correct. And everybody else's body tells me that I am correct. We never stop to consider what the original cause of all of our perception is, and certainly never stop to consider what the original cause of all of our judgments are.

(M-8.5:1-2) There can be no order of difficulty in healing merely because all sickness is illusion. Is it harder to dispel the belief of the insane in a larger hallucination as opposed to a smaller one?

What this is really talking about is what the title of this section is. It is about order of difficulties, which is another way of saying that there is no order of difficulty in miracles. There is no order of difficulty because one illusion is like any other illusion. Whether my eye has gone blind or I simply have a speck of dirt in it, it is the exact same problem. Both of them come from the same cause, which is a decision of my mind to exclude the vision of Christ, the decision of my mind to identify with the ego instead of with the Holy Spirit.

(M-8.5:3-5) Will he agree more quickly to the unreality of a louder voice he hears than to that of a softer one? Will he dismiss more easily a whispered demand to kill than a shout? And do the number of pitchforks the devils he sees carrying affect their credibility in his perception?

In other words, one times zero is the same as a thousand times zero. A headache is the same thing as AIDS. Because both of them come from the belief that the body is real, that guilt is real, that conflict is real and that God is not real. What heals all of the problems in the exact same way is to bring the illusion, to bring the form of the problem back to the cause. There is only one cause.

There are thousands and millions of effects. There are thousands and millions and hundreds of thousands and hundreds of thousands, millions, of symptoms and problems. But there is still only one cause. Dealing with the effects doesn't change what the cause is. It is only bringing the effect or the problem back to the cause that can help. And there is only one cause—the cause in the belief in sin. When we undo that cause, all problems disappear regardless of their seeming magnitude. That is the judgment that we are asked to make. That is the only judgment. Not only is it the only judgment we are asked to make, it is the only judgment that we can make in this world that makes sense.

Q: So when our perception changes, our problems all disappear?

A: Yes. Well, the form may not disappear. But the problem will disappear. Because the problem is not the form; the problem is the belief in the form.

(M-8.5:6) His mind has categorized them all as real, and so they are all real to him.

While Jesus is using the example of someone who is psychotic, someone whom we say is clinically insane, obviously we all fit into that category. We may not be clinically insane, but we're all insane. Because remember, the definition of insanity is when we make what reality is into illusion, and we make illusion into reality. Clearly, that is what we have all done. Those people we judge as being clinically insane or psychotic are merely further along in that same delusion. There is a quantitative difference but not really a qualitative one.

(M-8.5:7-9) When he realizes they are all illusions they will disappear. And so it is with healing. The properties of

illusions which seem to make them different are really irrelevant, for their properties are as illusory as they are.

Again what this is talking about is the difference between form and content. Within the ego system, there is only one content, and that is sin or guilt or fear. It is unreal, because only love is reality. Everything else, all the other forms, come from that one basic content. So again, on a specific level, on a practical level in our experience, we live in a world where everybody seems different. And we make judgments, whether they are conscious or not, of who can best serve our needs.

Those people who can best serve our needs are those people we pay attention to. They become the special figures in our ground. Those people whom we don't need, who can't help us in any way, then those people we put into the background. Those people who meet my needs today are the people that I am attracted to and I pay attention to. And if they stop meeting my needs, then I discard them. But everybody is judged based upon form, and everybody is judged as being different.

The difference or the basis of the judgment I make is what my particular need is. The answer to all that from the Holy Spirit's point of view is to realize that we are all the same. There are certain people whom we have to learn our lessons with. Those are the special functions that the Course talks about. But that doesn't mean because this person, let's say who's in my family, who obviously will be a learning lesson for me as opposed to someone else whom I don't know—it doesn't mean that person is better or worse than anyone else. It simply means that is the person I've chosen to be in my classroom. But it is not based upon value, good versus bad.

(M-8.6:1-2) The body's eyes will continue to see differences. But the mind that has let itself be healed will no longer acknowledge them.

This is extremely important. This is the idea that we have been discussing a lot this weekend. In other words, we are not asked in the Course to deny what our eyes see. We are not asked to deny all the differences that appear so real to us in the world. Likewise, we are not asked to deny all the ego feelings that we have—feelings of sickness, feelings of guilt, feelings of anger, feelings of anxiety. That is a real mistake a lot of students of the Course get into.

For example, they will say the Course says sickness is a defense against the truth. Therefore, I am not sick even though I have a fever of 103. Or they'll say, well my nose has a cold but I don't have a cold because I am a good student of *A Course in Miracles* and therefore, I cannot have a cold. That is not what this is talking about. What it is saying is that our body's eyes will continue to see differences. We will continue to feel differences. But I will be aware, for example, that one moment I was feeling loving and peaceful and the next moment I was feeling angry.

I am not asked to deny the fact that I am angry. Rather, what I am asked to do is to go back in my mind and look at that with Jesus or the Holy Spirit next to me and say, "Oh, a moment ago, I was feeling wonderful and peaceful and happy. I became afraid of that feeling. I became afraid of my closeness to you and so quickly I chose a defense against your love." I became angry, I became sick, I became anxious, depressed, etc. But I don't deny the difference that I am feeling, whether it is a difference that I am perceiving in you or a difference I am perceiving in myself.

I don't acknowledge them. Now what this means again, and the difference here is important. My body's eyes continue to see differences, but my mind no longer acknowledges them, which means my mind no longer acknowledges them as real. Jesus perceived what people were doing to him on the cross. But his mind did not acknowledge what they were doing as real. In other words, his mind did not acknowledge and did not experience any effect of what people were doing to him.

We are not asked to deny our physical or psychological experience in the world. What we are asked to do is take that belief that something on the outside is real—and it is real because it has an effect on me—that is how I know it is real, or I've made it real—and recognize this has no reality because it has no power to take away God's peace if I choose to acknowledge God's peace within me. So again, we are not asked to deny what we experience in the world. We are simply asked to give it a different interpretation.

Or to say it another way, we are not asked to deny what happens in the world, but to understand it differently and give it a different judgment. The ego's judgment is, this is a victimizing thing. This is a victimizing person; this is a victimizing activity; this is a victimizing phenomenon that is going on. The Holy Spirit's judgment is, "How can a Son of God be victimized by anything? A Son of God can only be victimized by anything if he forgets he's a Son of God, and believes rather that he's a son of the ego." That is the difference in judgment.

(M-8.6:3) There will be those who seem to be "sicker" than others, and the body's eyes will report their changed appearances as before.

So again, we are not asked to say that someone who has cancer is not sicker than someone who has a mild headache. We are not asked to deny that. Our body's eyes will still see it that way.

(M-8.6:4) But the healed mind will put them all in one category; they are unreal.

In a very specific and practical level, what that means is that regardless of having a headache or having cancer, regardless of having lost a dollar in the subway or lost a thousand dollars in the subway, the peace of God is still within me. That is why they are unreal. Whatever it is that happens outside, whatever it is you do, has absolutely no effect on the love and the peace of God that is within me. Nothing that you do has the power to disrupt or take away from my relationship with Jesus.

If it seems to, it is not because of what you've done. It is because I first made the decision to separate myself from his love, and then I blame you for it. Just as, right at the beginning, we all made a decision to separate ourselves from God's Love and then we blamed Him for it. And we say the reason this happened was because He attacked me first, He stole from me; and therefore, I am justified in stealing back from Him. And then He feels justified in punishing me, and it is not fair because He started it.

Again, this is what this is saying. To say that it is unreal, the world is unreal, is not to deny our physical or psychological experience here. That is a confusion of levels. Rather, what we are asked to do is to deny that anything anyone does has the power to disrupt or take away or detract from the love and the peace of God within. And that is the judgment.

(M-8.6:5-6) This is the gift of its Teacher; [this is the gift of the mind's Teacher with a capital "T"] **the understanding that only two categories are meaningful in sorting out the messages the mind receives from what appears to be the outside world.** [And there are only two messages: there is love or fear; God or the ego.] **And of these two, but one is real.**

The ego obviously is what is unreal. The ego's messages seem to be messages of victimization, of suffering, of pain, of hatred, of evil, of sin. The Holy Spirit doesn't deny what we have seen. He reinterprets it as being a call for love. Therefore, "Only two categories are meaningful in sorting out the messages" of the world translates into something is either an expression of love or else it is a call for it.

(M-8.6:7) Just as reality is wholly real, apart from size and shape and time and place—for differences cannot exist within it—[That is a statement of what Heaven is. There are no differences within Heaven. God and Christ are not different.] **so too are illusions without distinctions.**

All illusions are exactly the same because they come from the same cause. You take away the cause of sin, which means we don't take it seriously, we don't acknowledge it has any effects. All the effects must disappear. The effects are not necessarily the effects in form. The effects are guilt, anxiety, terror, sadness, loneliness, fear, etc., etc. Those will disappear.

(M-8.6:8-9) The one answer to sickness of any kind is healing. The one answer to all illusions is truth.

Are Changes Required in the Life Situation of God's Teachers?

If we just look at the bottom of page 26, the end of that section. We will do the whole second paragraph on that page.

(M-9.2:1-2) As the teacher of God advances in his training, [This by the way is a clear expression of the idea that within the world of dreams, within the world of illusions, you do make progress, and there are gradations.] **he learns one lesson with increasing thoroughness. He does not make his own decisions; he asks his Teacher for His answer, and it is this he follows as his guide for action.**

Now here, too, this doesn't mean that you necessarily have to stop what you are doing to meditate, pray and then ask the Holy Spirit what you should do, and wait for His Voice and do what He tells you. That is not what this is talking about. What it is talking about is a process whereby we realize that it is our investment in outcomes, it is our judgments that interfere with our hearing God's Voice.

When the Course talks about hearing the Holy Spirit's Voice, it doesn't necessarily mean hearing it on the level of form, that people will experience a voice just as Helen did when she heard Jesus' voice and wrote down the Course. That is one way of experiencing the Holy Spirit or Jesus, but there are thousands and thousands of other ways. All the forms are just different forms of the same content. It is the content which is important, not the form.

All the forms are illusory. To talk about the Holy Spirit as a voice is an illusion. It is not really a voice. The Holy Spirit is a presence of love, which is abstract. How we experience the Holy Spirit's answer is totally individualized and there is no higher or lower way of doing it.

(M-9.2:3) This becomes easier and easier, as the teacher of God learns to give up his own judgment.

This is another clear statement, if you really read it carefully, that all that we are asked to do to hear the Holy Spirit's Voice, all that we are asked to do to be in the presence of God's Love and peace, is to give up judgment. That line I began with Friday night, that we have no idea of the deep peace that will come to us when we give up judgment. It is our judgment (which is just another way of saying, our adhering to the ego's thought system of difference and separation) that is what the problem is. We don't have to strain to hear the Holy Spirit's Voice. We don't have to meditate hours and hours to hear the Holy Spirit's Voice.

All we have to do is give up our investment in being right. All we have to do is give up our investment in judgment. That is all we have to do. The Voice will automatically come at that point. Just as when I discussed earlier today about joining. You don't have to do anything to join. You simply undo the investment and the belief in being separate. You don't have to do anything to hear the Holy Spirit's Voice, because His presence is already there. His love is already in our mind. We have simply covered it over. One way to describe the coverings to conceal His voice, is judgment.

(M-9.2:4) The giving up of judgment, the obvious prerequisite for hearing God's Voice, is usually a fairly slow process....

I think if you have highlighters, you should highlight that in yellow, pink, green, blue. Pass them around so everybody gets it. The reason I say that is because people work with this course and have the illusion that you can just do this course in one year and you are home. There is a line in the Course that says never underestimate the power of the ego (T-5.V.2:11). Our identification with the ego is very, very strong because our fear of God's punishment is enormous. So this is:

(M-9.2:4) ... usually a fairly slow process, not because it is difficult but because it is apt to be perceived as personally insulting.

Obviously, that is insulting to the ego. The ego doesn't like to be told it is wrong. Because we are all so sure that we are right. We know the right way or the best way of doing whatever it is that we think it is. Whatever it is we think we are expert in, we know. And then we feel that it is personally insulting to be told that we are wrong or that someone has a different opinion. As if it really matters.

The whole point of everything we have been talking about is that it doesn't matter. We are just talking about different forms of an illusion. What difference does it make if it is red or green or big or tall, or a blue book or a green book? It doesn't matter if you are right or if you are wrong. All that matters is that you recognize it doesn't matter, and that the one thing that does matter is the love of God.

(M-9.2:5) The world's training is directed toward achieving a goal in direct opposition to that of our curriculum.

Obviously, we are the ones who told the world how to train us. It is really not that the world trains us. It is not that the world trains us to be sick egos. It is our sick egos that made up a world that then appears to be training us. But the training that the world gives us, which again is what we have first given the world, is to judge. We know how to judge right from wrong, good from evil, what will make us happy, what will make us sad. We judge pleasure from pain, etc., etc.

(M-9.2:6-7) The world trains for reliance on one's judgment as the criterion for maturity and strength. Our curriculum trains for the relinquishment of judgment as the necessary condition of salvation.

Is Psychotherapy a Profession?

There is a parallel idea in the *Psychotherapy* pamphlet on page 18. I'm reading in the second paragraph of that.

(P-3.II.2) First, the professional therapist is in an excellent position to demonstrate that there is no order of difficulty in healing. For this, however, he needs special training, because the curriculum by which he became a therapist probably taught him little or nothing about the real principles of healing. In fact, it probably taught him how to make healing impossible. [He's not hot on psychotherapists, by the way.] **Most of the world's teaching follows a curriculum in judgment, with the aim of making the therapist a judge.**

That is the exact same thing. And then on the next page it says:

(P-3.II.6:1) It is in the instant that the therapist forgets to judge the patient that healing occurs.

Again, it is our judgments that stand in the way of healing. All that healing is, is the acceptance of the love and the unity and the truth that is within everyone's mind. It is all one Mind.

We are all different parts of the one Mind. Judgment obviously excludes and separates out.

Raising Children

Q: Would you advise raising children along the lines of this?

A: The answer is, that you don't raise children. That is the fallacy of your question. Because your question is really asking, how do you raise children. Or should I raise children this way or that way. The answer is that you don't raise children. Because you don't do anything. All that you do is you bring to the Holy Spirit all of your preconceptions about raising children, and He's the one who raises children. Which means there is no right way or wrong way of raising children.

There is a right way or wrong way of looking at your mind, or a right way or a wrong way of thinking or perceiving. But there is not a right way or a wrong way of doing anything. And there is not *A Course in Miracles* way of doing it. That if you are *A Course in Miracles* student and you now find yourself a parent, you don't ask the Holy Spirit, how to be the best parent I can be. Because then what you are doing is making the error real.

What you do is you realize that you've become a parent because that is a classroom you have chosen in which you learn the same lessons everybody learns, regardless of the form. All that you want to do is bring to the Holy Spirit all of your guilt, all of your anxiety, all of your special love, all of your special hate—all the things that go into being a parent. Bring that to Him and in a sense say, I don't know what I should do, I don't know what the most loving thing is to do, and I don't care.

All I want to do is be with Your love and I know that Your love will come through me, and Your love will then dictate what it is I do as a parent, as a friend, as a spouse, as a child, as a this, as a that. Otherwise, you'll get caught, you see. Then we are trying to do the form the right way. There is no *Course in Miracles'* way of doing anything on the level of form. There is only an attitude that *A Course in Miracles* fosters.

How Is Judgment Relinquished?

Let's turn to page 27 in the teacher's manual. Let's start with the second paragraph.

(M-10.2:1-6) It is necessary for the teacher of God to realize, not that he should not judge, but that he cannot. [And again, we cannot judge because it is the ego in us that is judging.] **In giving up judgment, he is merely giving up what he did not have. He gives up an illusion; or better, he has an illusion of giving up. He has actually merely become more honest. Recognizing that judgment was always impossible for him, he no longer attempts it. This is no sacrifice.**

What Jesus is really saying is, you should give up judgment not because I am asking you to, not because I am a better judge than you; simply because you cannot judge and I am the only judge, or the Holy Spirit is the only judge. Rather than see this as an insult, we should take it with a sigh of welcome relief.

(M-10.2:7-9) On the contrary, he puts himself in a position where judgment *through* him rather than *by* him can occur. And this judgment is neither "good" nor "bad." It is the only judgment there is, and it is only one: "God's Son is guiltless, and sin does not exist."

Q: I had a situation I encountered when I first started the Course three years ago. I was called for jury duty. What do you do in a situation like that, where you have to make a decision one way or the other?

142

A: It's exactly the same. It's exactly the same as Tom's question about parenting, or Jim's question about the guy who cuts you off. It is no different. In other words, what you do is you go to the jury because that is what a citizen does in this world. If you are called for jury duty, you go serve on the jury. You go to the jury and you say to the Holy Spirit, obviously, this is a classroom I have chosen to learn lessons, and now I will bring to you all of the feelings that this is bringing up, such as, I am a good *Course in Miracles* student, the Course says I shouldn't judge and how could I judge? And the Holy Spirit will say, silly, silly. That is not what I meant.

What I meant was that everything in this world is silly. So He says, don't sweat the small stuff. Sit on that jury and bring to me all of your concerns and then I will tell you how to vote. And you will vote guilty or not guilty. But this has nothing to do with content. It only has to do with form. On the level of form, people are guilty or not guilty. As a citizen living in a world of form, then if you are on a jury, you make the decision based on whatever it is that you base it on. This person is guilty of the crime as charged or is not guilty. In your heart you know that everyone is not guilty in Heaven; and everybody is guilty here. Everybody is guilty and not guilty at the same time. So what is the big deal?

If you listen carefully, that is what Jesus or the Holy Spirit would say to you every single time you come to Him with a problem. He'll say, what is the big deal? You are upset by something that is not there. And you are using what is not there as a way of keeping hidden from you what is truly there. And that is what you are doing. What you are keeping hidden from you, what is truly there, is my love. That is what you are afraid of. So you hide that. What you hide it with is what is not there and then you make-believe that you are upset about it. Again, that is what makes this course so simple. Because everything falls into that category.

Q: But then there is a decision of wanting to study *A Course in Miracles.* Isn't that a decision?

A: Yes. But it could either be a reflection of a decision of the ego or a decision of the Holy Spirit. Someone could choose to study *A Course in Miracles* as a magical attempt at saying now I have God right where I want Him. I am going to do exactly what He says in this book and then He's going to have to forgive me and love me. And then people are absolutely faithful to doing the workbook and they read the text faithfully and they attend their *Course in Miracles* groups faithfully and they pray for all the sick people in the world and do everything they think they are supposed to do, and nothing has happened.

Choosing to study the Course is the same thing as choosing to become a parent or serve on a jury or to have a lamb chop. Shakespeare said that the devil can cite scripture for its own purpose. Well, the Course says the ego can use the Course for its own purpose, too. The Course is only a form. The form is neutral. It can either serve the purpose of the ego or the purpose of the Holy Spirit. One could read the telephone book and be healed. You could read all the names in the telephone book and say, they are all the same. They seem to be different; and they are all the same. You got it. Right there. That sounds much, much easier than wading through these three books. (laughter) Do you think we should close the Foundation, honey? (More laughter) But it is no different.

Let's turn to page 28, second paragraph.

(M-10.5:1-2) Therefore lay judgment down, not with regret but with a sigh of gratitude. Now are you free of a burden so great that you could merely stagger and fall down beneath it.

I think if we really stop to consider the tremendous burden and tremendous weight that judgment is, we would gladly give it up. The idea that we always have to know the right answer. And we take seriously that we have to know the right answer. That we believe that decisions that we make really count for something.

One of the worst things that can happen to a parent is believing that something I do with my three-year-old child is going to affect that child for the rest of his or her life. That is absurd. But most people actually fall into that trap, because psychology teaches the child is the father of the man. By the time the child is six, everything is written. And his fate is sealed. I would better be really good for those first six years. Or to believe that if I am a pregnant mother and I take a cigarette or I take a drink, that I am adversely affecting the fetus. Or if I have negative thoughts, that is adversely affecting the fetus. I mean that is a terrible, terrible burden, what I do or say affects somebody else.

And where does that come from? The original belief that my thought about being separate from God had a terrible effect. Look at the effect it had. This entire world, which is a world of suffering, pain and misery, is the effect of that one single thought—that tiny, mad idea. And that is deeply buried in the consciousness of everyone. My thought had the power to destroy Heaven and make this whole world, which is a place of suffering and death, and I did it.

When I have a thought about saying something to my child and I become guilty about it, what is happening there is that that becomes the reminder that what I am doing is going to have an adverse effect on this child, because look at what my thought did to God and to Christ. And to believe that judgment is real for us and that our judgments have effects comes from that same idea. It is an awful, awful burden. That is why everybody walks around so guilt-laden and so miserable and unhappy. We have little glimmers of light every once in awhile, but it never lasts. The good news is that our thoughts have no effect at all. They have an effect if I believe in them. But then the problem is not the thoughts or the effects, but the fact that I believe in them.

(M-10.5:5-7) Now can the teacher of God rise up unburdened, and walk lightly on. Yet it is not only this that is his benefit. His sense of care is gone, for he has none.

It means you stop caring about yourself, you stop caring about everybody else. Caring is not a happy thing. Caring is not a loving thing. Caring does not come from the Holy Spirit. Caring comes from the ego. It comes from making a judgment that somebody has to be cared for. Caring comes from a judgment that I can care for you better than God can care for you. I can care for you better than Jesus can care for you. Caring comes from the idea that I am God and I am the one who can do all this. I know what is best for you and I know how to give it to you. Caring is not loving. Caring comes from a perception of someone else as being weak, as being an ego. Caring comes from a perception of differences; that is what the judgment is. You are in need of help and I am the one who can help you. Again, we are not talking about the level of form; we are talking about an attitude.

(M-10.5:8-12) He has given it away, [in other words, he has given care away] **along with judgment. He gave himself to Him Whose judgment he has chosen now to trust, instead of his own. Now he makes no mistakes. His Guide is sure. And where he came to judge, he comes to bless. Where now he laughs, he used to come to weep.**

When one listens to the voice of the ego, one can only weep at this world. The laughter in this world is simply a cover for the weeping and the sadness and the tears that is underneath. If you really look at this world for what it is, it is a place of great sadness. It is a world of loss, of abandonment, of pain, of suffering and of death. It is not a happy place. When one looks at it through the eyes of the Holy Spirit, everything is seen as a classroom. Everything is seen as an illusion, which means again not that you deny what happens on the level of form, but you deny that it has any power to take away your peace. And that is what enables you to laugh at it. Whether he actually physically laughed or not, unquestionably in his mind, Jesus laughed on the cross. Because nothing was happening to him.

(M-10.6:1-2) It is not difficult to relinquish judgment. But it is difficult indeed to try to keep it.

This is another important thought in the Course. Jesus keeps telling us it is much, much easier to accept what is true than to deny it. Since everyone in this world and everything in this world is the denial of truth, we all work very, very hard. That is why we all get tired and experience fatigue. It is much more difficult to attempt to deny what is there, and cover it over and keep covering it over and covering it over, than it is to simply let go of all the covers and say there is nothing here except love. And basically, that is what Jesus is trying to teach us in the Course.

It is much easier, and you'll be much happier, doing what I tell you to do than to try to drown out my voice and do what you tell you to do. Because that requires tremendous effort. To deny something that is there, if you think about it, requires a great deal of effort. It required tremendous effort and ingenuity to develop a complex theology to try to deny that God is simply love. All you really have to say is God is love. And that is it. The Course says you say the words "God is" and you cease to speak. (W.pI.169.5:4)

But to try to deny God's Love by inventing a god who believes in suffering and pain and sacrifice and crucifixion and vengeance, etc., requires a lot of work. As you read the five laws of chaos in chapter 23, they are very, very complicated and very difficult. Because it takes a complicated system to drown out what is so simple. God Is. That is all you say. The introduction to the text says, "Nothing real can be threatened. Nothing unreal exists. Herein lies the peace of God" (T-in.2: 2-4). It is very, very simple.

What is false is false, what is true has never changed (W-pII.10.1:1). That is very simple. Truth is, and nothing else is at all. That is very simple. But the world is extremely complicated. And we invent very complicated theologies, philosophies, psychologies, etc., etc., all attempting to disguise what is so simple and obvious. That is what he's saying here. It is not difficult to give up judgment. It is extremely difficult to try to hold onto it. It requires tremendous effort. It requires great effort to always push the love of God away.

(M-10.6:3) The teacher of God lays it down happily the instant he recognizes its cost.

And this is the idea. Just as we have been talking about, using Jim's example again of a driver cutting you off, and you feel yourself getting annoyed or getting angry, you simply look at the anger and you say I am choosing the anger to keep the peace of God away from me. Is this really what I want? In other words, the cost of my anger is I have lost the peace of God. Is that really what I want? No matter how justified I feel in feeling unfairly treated and feeling victimized, is it really worth it to me to give up that wonderful feeling of knowing that God's love was within me? And yet that is what we are always doing without realizing that is what we are doing.

(M-10.6:4-6) All of the ugliness he sees about him is its outcome [the outcome of judgment]. **All of the pain he looks upon is its result. All of the loneliness and sense of loss; of passing time and growing hopelessness; of sickening despair and fear of death; all these have come of it.**

What Jesus is saying to us, look at the effects of our decision to judge, and say, "Is this really what we want?" When if we let go of judgment, what we will have is the peace of God.

At the end of chapter 23, which is also the chapter where the laws of chaos is found, it says, "Who with the Love of God upholding him could find the choice of miracles or murder hard to make?" (T-23.IV.9:8) Well, there is no question. When you can see clearly that the choice is between the miracle, which is what the peace of God is, or murder, nobody would hesitate. Everybody would immediately choose the peace of God if we knew that is what we were really choosing. And that murder was really murder.

The problem is that we don't know that. We confuse the two. There are parallel sections in the text, "The Confusion of Pain and Joy" (T-7.X) and "The Difference between Imprisonment and Freedom" (T-8.II). The problem is we don't know the difference. What we believe is pain is really joy. What we believe is joy is really pain. Because to the ego, obscuring God's Love and attacking it is its greatest joy. What we think will imprison us, which is to be back in God's arms, is really freedom. What we believe is freedom, which is to be free and independent in this world and to express my individuality, etc., etc.—that is really imprisonment. Because it makes my separated self very real. I have a thought; I have a feeling. Isn't that wonderful? I have an opinion. Isn't that wonderful? But it's I. I, I, I—instead of we.

(M-10.6:7) And now he knows that these things need not be.

There is a section early on in the text that is called, "This Need Not Be" (T-4.IV), which goes into all of the things that need not be in terms of depression, despair, pain, etc.

(M-10.6:8) Not one is true.

Now that means if none of these things is true—loneliness, sense of loss, despair, death, etc.—if none of these effects is true, then their cause cannot be true. The cause then is judgment, which means judgment is not true. And that is why Jesus says it's not that you shouldn't judge. It's that you cannot judge.

(M-10.6:9-11) For he has given up their cause, and they, which never were but the effects of his mistaken choice,

have fallen from him. Teacher of God, this step will bring you peace. Can it be difficult to want but this?

Well, of course, it is not difficult. But the ego has told us—which is another way of understanding its original judgment, that if you go back to the peace of God, if you embrace the voice of the Holy Spirit and accept His love and His Atonement principle, you will be destroyed. Because we believed that one judgment and never, ever questioned it again, we then are always trying to avoid the peace of God and avoid love and avoid joining and avoid forgiving. Because to our disturbed and insane mind, we believe that will destroy us.

We no longer see the connection between our stubbornly holding onto that premise and all of the misery that we feel. We feel the misery is because of what happens outside of us. Once again, that is the basis for all of our judgments. I want to judge the world outside as good or bad, as victim or victimizer, because that is what allows my mind to get off the hook. I don't have to go back within to look at the one judgment that I made, which was judging to join the ego instead of the Holy Spirit.

What is the Last Judgment?

What I would like to do in the last part of the workshop is to talk about the concept in the Course of God's final judgment, or the Last Judgment. The Course uses the terms in two ways. Early on in the text, there is a section on the last judgment, which is reinterpreted by Jesus from the traditional Christian understanding. The traditional Christian understanding of the last judgment is that it is carried out by God at the end of time and it is the last judgment of separating the sheep from the goats, the good people from the bad people. There is a famous parable in Matthew where Jesus gives the parable of the last judgment, where he talks about the sheep and the goats. Obviously, that is a concept that has fear built into it. Everybody is trying to strike a special bargain with God to be among the sheep instead of among the goats. I want to do what You want me to do so You won't be angry at me.

One of the ways of understanding our need to project guilt onto other people and judge against them, with great justification, is to hold the person's head up, drag him to God and say I found the sinner, and it is not me. It is this other person. I am innocent; there is the sinner, right there. In Your last judgment, he's the goat and I am the sheep. What Jesus does in the Course, especially in that section called "The Meaning of the Last Judgment," (T.2.VIII) is reinterpret it to be the last judgment is not carried out by God. It is carried out by us. And it is the final judgment of the collective Son of God that has been awakened from the dream.

It also talks about the second coming as being when all the seemingly separated fragments of the Sonship reunite. Every last fragment has accepted the Atonement for himself. We are all now reunited as one mind. We then make the final, or the last judgment that everything in the world is illusory. Everything of God is true. That is the last judgment. It is the final separating out of the true from the false. That ends the whole Atonement plan and then it says God takes the final step Himself and reaches down and lifts us back unto Himself (W-pI.168.3:2).

But the Course also uses the term final judgment or God's judgment to denote what God's judgment of us is really is, which is that we are His beloved Son, and that nothing has happened. What I would actually like to read from now is in the workbook on page 455. It is the page that answers the question, "What is the Last Judgment?" (W-pII.10). What we find on this page is basically the last judgment or the final judgment from the point of view of the Sonship, as well as the Final Judgment of God.

(W-pII.10.1:1) Christ's Second Coming gives the Son of God this gift ....

The Second Coming of Christ is basically the undoing of what happened after the First Coming. The First Coming of Christ is the creation of Christ. Then it appeared as if the Son of God fell asleep and had this awful dream. And then the awakening from that dream is the Second Coming. The Second Coming really is the undoing of the separation, which was the ego's answer to the First Coming. So this is the gift that the Second Coming brings to us.

(W-pII.10.1:1) ... to hear the Voice for God proclaim that what is false is false, and what is true has never changed.

That basically is what the Holy Spirit told us right at the beginning. His loving presence in our mind is the reminder that only God is true, that we have never left our Father's house, the separation was nothing but a bad dream, what is true has never changed. We have not changed Heaven, we have not changed God, we have not changed love. God has not changed His Mind about us. And what is false is simply false. The tiny, mad idea that seemed to arise within the mind of the Sonship that we could be separate from God and judge against Him, never happened.

(W-pII.10.1:2) And this the judgment is in which perception ends.

Perception was made by the ego because perception involves judgment and it involves differences. There is an object that is perceived and there is a perceiver. There is subject and object; there is a difference. There is separation. That is what the ego made. The Holy Spirit then corrects the perceptions of judgment by introducing His judgment, which as we have seen, is either someone is calling for love or expressing love. But there is no condemnation in that. That is what true perception is.

(W-pII.10.1:3) At first you see a world that has accepted this as true, [in other words, what is false is false, and what is true has never changed] **projected from a now corrected mind.**

That is what the real world is. My mind has been healed. As I look out on the world, I still see bodies. I still see what is out here. But I say what is true has never changed and what is false is false. Which means all the forms that I am perceiving here are false. They are just flimsy veils that can no longer hide the truth of the light of Christ that shines in you. And that is what we all perceive once our minds are healed.

That is the way Jesus walked this earth. He saw what everybody else saw on the level of form. But his judgment was, what is false is false, and what is true has never changed. When he hung from the cross, what was false was his body. Nothing happened. What is true about him, the light of Christ and the love of God within him, within his mind, had never changed. And his message, of course, to us was not one of suffering and sacrifice and guilt and vengeance. His message to us was, look at me and realize what is false is false, and what is true has never changed. And what is true about me is also true about you.

(W-pII.10.1:4) And with this holy sight, perception gives a silent blessing and then disappears, its goal accomplished and its mission done.

That would be the end of the world and the end of the whole Atonement path.

(W-pII.10.2:1-2) The final judgment on the world contains no condemnation. For it sees the world as totally forgiven, without sin and wholly purposeless.

The real world is still part of the illusion. But the Course explains that it is the second part of the hallucination. The first part is that this world is real and it is awful. The second part of the hallucination is that the world is not awful and it is not real. But we still perceive a world. It is like being in a dream at night but being aware that you are dreaming. We see the world, but there is no thought of sin, there is no thought of separation. And my body's eyes perceive differences, but my experience is, we are all one.

There is no anger. There is no guilt. There is no judgment. There is total acceptance. You see people's egos, but you don't attack them. You don't judge them. You don't give up the judgment that allows us to live in this world. You don't deny that people do all kinds of funny things. You just don't judge them for it, which means no matter what people do, it has no effect on your love for them.

Again, that is another way of understanding what the message of the crucifixion was. No matter what the world did to Jesus, his love for the world was totally unchanged. And that is the message we are asked to give to each of us. That is what he means when he asks us to be his manifestation in the world. No matter what you do, no matter what your ego has done, it has no effect on my love for you.

(W-pII.10.2:3) Without a cause, and now without a function in Christ's sight, [and this is the world that it is talking about] **it merely slips away to nothingness.**

As the manual says, the world slips away, back into the nothingness from which it came. Because that is all the world was. The world is the effect of that tiny, mad idea of being separate from God. When that thought is undone, then the world is undone, too.

(W-pII.10.2:4-5) There it was born, [the world was born in nothingness—it is the nothingness of the ego thought system] **and there it ends as well. And all the figures in the dream in which the world began go with it.**

All the belief in separate bodies, all the belief in separate things, all disappear. Because all the separate things are simply the effect of the separate thought. But there was no separate thought. There was just a belief there was a separate thought. We change the belief in the reality of that separate thought and everything else disappears as well.

(W-pII.10.2:6) Bodies now are useless, and will therefore fade away, because the Son of God is limitless.

Once again, as I think we talked about earlier, this does not mean that when you forgive, your body will go poof. What it means is that when you forgive, your belief in bodies as important will go poof. Your investment in bodies will go poof. Your investment in the body as a source of pleasure and pain will go poof. Your depression, your guilt, your anxiety, your tension—all of those will go poof. It is not that the body will go poof. All the ego thoughts and all the pain of living here will go poof.

(W-pII.10.3:1) You who believed that God's Last Judgment would condemn the world to hell along with you, accept this holy truth....

And obviously, this is everyone. This is not just people who grew up as Christians. All that Christianity did was take the underlying thought that is in everybody's mind and raise it to the level of theology and to truth. But everyone believes this. Because if we didn't, then we wouldn't be here. First of all, we chose to make this world, and then to come into it to hide from God's judgment. That is why we are all here. Again, all that religions have done and Christianity in particular has done, is take the ego thoughts and elevate them into the word of God. This is what the truth really is.

(W-pII.10.3:1) God's Judgment is the gift of the Correction He bestowed on all of your errors, [Correction is capitalized, which means that it refers to the Holy Spirit] **freeing you from them, and all effects they ever seemed to have.**

The Holy Spirit's use of judgment is to separate out what is true from what is false. And what is true is that anything in this world not only is unreal, but it has no power over me. We are not asked to accept and to experience what the Course is teaching us metaphysically; namely, that this whole world is a dream. Because obviously, we still believe that we are bodies.

What we are asked to do is to deny that the dream has any effect on us. And the way that we do that is to practice every single day in terms of our experiences. The practicing obviously extends far beyond the one-year workbook period. It is the practicing all of the time. And what the practicing is, is when I find myself tempted to be upset by something, to realize I am not upset by what is outside. I am upset by a decision I made inside to keep God's Love away from me.

(W-pII.10:3:2) To fear God's saving grace is but to fear complete release from suffering, return to peace, security and happiness, and union with your own Identity.

This obviously is what the ego told us right at the beginning. That we should be afraid of peace, of security and happiness and reuniting with our Self. Because the ego told us, if we do all of this, God will destroy us. And so God's saving grace, which would be the presence of the Holy Spirit's love in our mind, is seen as the enemy. And that is the ego's judgment against God, which we identify with, and then we are off and running.

(W-pII.10.4:1-2) God's Final Judgment is as merciful as every step in His appointed plan to bless His Son, and call him to return to the eternal peace He shares with him. Be not afraid of love.

That line is also a biblical line which is found in the Old Testament and is repeated many times by Jesus in the gospels. The reason it is so important is that we are obviously afraid of love. We are afraid of the love of God in our mind, and we are obviously afraid of love in this world. We are afraid of really giving up attack thoughts and anger thoughts. We are really afraid of giving up judgments. We are really afraid of joining with people on the level of content, and insist that it is form that is important.

Whenever we find ourselves insisting we are right, we should try to step back and say, by my insistence that I am right, I am really giving up the love and the peace that I could experience right now. Because whenever I am insisting I am right, I must be insisting somebody else is wrong. As I mentioned yesterday, I would never be so insistent on being right if I were not convinced within me that I was wrong. And that I tried to deny what I really feel about myself and say no, I am not wrong, I am right. In fact, I am not right, I am always right. And all of that again is a defense against God's Love.

(W-pII.10.4:3) For it alone [God's Love alone] **can heal all sorrow, wipe away all tears, and gently waken from his dream of pain the Son whom God acknowledges as His.**

Now the ego, of course, tells us that I can wipe away all your tears. And I can wipe away all your sorrow. I can end all of your pain, and it is very simple. You just beat the hell out of everybody else. That is how you avoid pain in this world. You project the cause onto other people and you attack them.

(W-pII.10.4:4-6) Be not afraid of this. [In other words, be not afraid of God's Love that will truly awaken us from the dream of pain and end all of our problems here.] **Salvation asks you give it welcome. And the world awaits your glad acceptance, which will set it free.**

Salvation is already present in our mind. All that we are asked to do is welcome it. There is a line right near the end of the workbook on page 479, which says at the end of the third paragraph:

(W-pII.14.3:7) We are concerned only with giving welcome to the truth.

That is what our concern is. Our concern is not the truth. Our concern is not salvation. Our concern is not God's Love. Our concern is simply giving welcome to what is already present within us, which means, again, as we have seen, simply taking away all the layers of judgment and of guilt that we have placed between ourselves and this love. What frees the world—and it is not talking about an external world—it is talking about the world of the Sonship within my mind, which is within everyone's mind. What frees the world is simply giving welcome to the freeing thought. And the freeing thought, again, would be "What is false is false and what is true has never changed (W-pII.10.1:1). Everything that my eyes perceive, everything on the level of form, is untrue. And all that is true is the love of God that I've been so afraid of.

Closing
What is the Last Judgment?

At the bottom of the page is God's Final Judgment, which I'll read. And then we will just spend a bit in quiet. And that'll be the end of the workshop. This basically, of course, is what the Holy Spirit was trying to tell us right from the beginning. The purpose of the Course is to remove all the barriers that we placed between ourselves and this Final Judgment, so that we can finally hear this and accept its truth.

(W-pII.10.5) This is God's Final Judgment: "You are still My holy Son, forever innocent, forever loving and forever loved, as limitless as your Creator, and completely

changeless and forever pure. Therefore awaken and return to Me. I am your Father and you are My Son."

Excerpted Questions
God's Love

The workshop ended with this meditation. The rest of this tape contains questions and discussions excerpted from the workshop. Some editing has been done. When a question was not fully audible, I repeated it. A few others were rephrased to help with clarity and brevity.

Ken responded to the comment of a participant who said that he felt that he was holding onto his judgments because essentially he was just very afraid of God's Love.

K: Yeah. And there is nothing in the Course again that would ask us to just kind of give up those things. There are a couple of lines that I think are helpful in this regard. One is where the Course says that the Holy Spirit doesn't take your special relationships away from you (T-17.IV.2:3). What he does is transform them. We are not asked to give up the things that we like or the people that we like. All that we are asked to do is to shift the purpose that we have given them (T-15.V.5).

And then there is another line that says, do not be afraid that you'll be lifted up and abruptly hurled into reality (T-16.VI.8:1). It won't be splat. You are not going to, as the saying goes, go poof and leave your body. It doesn't work that way. All that will happen as you practice this course is that you will feel better over a period of time. And that you will feel less angry, less judgmental, less sick, etc., etc.

Ken was asked to elaborate on what the experience of God's Love is.

K: I think once you try to explain what God's Love is, then you've lost it, which is why the Course doesn't explain it. Basically, as it says right at the beginning of the text in the introduction, that this is not a Course that aims at teaching the meaning of love because that is beyond what can be taught. But what it does aim at doing is teaching us to remove the interferences to the awareness of love's presence (T-in.1:6-7). God's Love is unlike anything in this world.

There is one passage in the workbook which talks about our trying to think back to a time—and it can be a very, very brief period of time, even a few seconds, when we felt totally at peace and felt no sense of fear. And then to multiply that a hundred times and a hundred times more. And then at that point, we just get the faintest glimmering of what the peace of God is (W-pI.107). There is no experience in this world that can approximate that.

So I think it is extremely difficult to talk about what the love of God is or the peace of God is, because it is not of this world. And there is nothing in this world that could describe it. And anything in this world that we think is love or that we think is peaceful is just, again, a faint, faint, glimmering of what the actual experience is.

Integrating the Course

Another question referred to the series of statements on page 90 in the text, beginning with "I must have decided wrongly, because I am not at peace" (T-5.VII.6:7). The questioner asked whether these statements can be used in any situation in which we feel ourselves upset, and that whatever the circumstances are—fear, anger, and so forth—we need to just simply say these statements and then go right on being upset.

K: Obviously, it is not just reading it; it is integrating it. What the core of that series of statements is on page 90 is that

I am the one who has decided this. And if I am not at peace, it is because I have decided wrongly. That is very important. I am aware that the cause of my not being at peace is not the subway car or the person cutting me off or my not having enough to eat or this or that. The cause is, I made the decision in my mind to be separate from God, and that was the wrong one. And I chose to identify with my ego instead of the Holy Spirit. And because I am the one who chose that, I can then just as easily make another choice.

The World is Totally Neutral

Another question raised was this: If one's thoughts are peaceful and loving thoughts, then shouldn't the external world also be peaceful and loving?

K: But the outside world is not peaceful and it is not awful. In other words, the outside world is nothing. The Course says the body doesn't do anything. It doesn't get sick; it doesn't get well. It doesn't live, it doesn't die. In the larger sense, the world isn't happy; the world isn't dreary. The world isn't filled with war; it is not filled with peace. The world is totally neutral. The peace that I experience in the world comes from my mind. I can be just as peaceful in a beautiful setting such as we have here or at Times Square in New York City. It is not that the world becomes more peaceful; it is that my mind has become more peaceful. And I will then experience the world differently.

The world around Jesus, certainly, at the end of his life was hardly peaceful. It was murderous. Right? But that doesn't mean that there were murderous thoughts in him. Because he did not experience it as murder. As he says at the beginning of chapter 6, which is a very important section that deals with the crucifixion, he says that in the eyes of the world, I was beaten, abandoned, betrayed, torn and finally killed, but this was not a perception that I shared (T-6.I.9). The world around him, externally, was hardly peaceful and hardly love filled.

But his mind was peaceful and his mind was love filled. So his experience of the world was that either people were calling for love or expressing love. All that he saw was love around him. Even though on the material level, obviously, people were filled with hate and fear and guilt and murder. It is a mistake to believe that if you do this course right, your external world will change. It might change. But it doesn't mean that you are flunking the Course if it doesn't change. What you learn is that it doesn't matter.

We all fall into the trap of trying to evaluate our progress based upon how things go externally. Often people who are up here will say well, that if this place really were following Jesus, that nothing would ever break down here. We wouldn't have a septic problem, we wouldn't have a plumbing problem. We wouldn't have any problem. Everything would have to be perfect. Why? I think that the criterion for how well we do here as a staff is the degree of peace that we have regardless of what happens around us. Otherwise, what you are doing is trying to evaluate what is inside based upon what is outside.

And of course, that is what judgment is. And that's what, in a sense, everything that we have been looking at so far is about, and what the whole Course is about. That we cannot judge. To believe that I could judge how well I am doing inside by judging what is happening outside is silly. That is why there is a passage in the text where Jesus says that what you have judged to be your greatest advances have been your greatest failures. And what you have judged to be your greatest retreats have been your greatest successes (T-18. V.1:6).

What he's really saying is that there is no way we can evaluate anything. There is no way I can evaluate what is happening in your life, and certainly there is no way I can evaluate what is happening in my life. Because our judgments are always based upon what the body's eyes see. The body's eyes will see and will know that the Foundation is doing God's work because there is never a septic problem and never a heating problem and never a plumbing problem.

Pleasure as the Other Side of Pain

Q: Earlier this morning, you said something about pleasure being the other side of pain.

A: Yes, I did say that.

Q: Is the pleasure that we feel in this world not of God? Can you differentiate between the pleasure and the happiness that we feel in our inner life and the one in outer life?

A: Yes. There is a line at the end of chapter 1 in the text that says the only real pleasure comes in doing God's Will (T-1. VII.1:4). That is the pleasure that comes when I no longer see my will as separate from God's. That is pleasure, that is happiness, that is peace. What the world calls pleasure and happiness almost always has something to do with the body. I am happy because I got what I wanted. I feel pleasure. My body feels pleasure. So that my happiness and my pleasure is directly related to what happens to my body, or what another body does. Which means that it is always based on a whim. Because at some point, I might get what I want; the next time, I won't get what I want. The real pleasure which comes in doing God's Will, is constant. Because once I identify with it and stay with it, then the pleasure and the peace and the happiness is always there.

Fear of Joining

Q: How come whenever I get close to someone or I am almost getting close to someone, whether it's a friend, a boyfriend, someone in my family—it's almost like buttons get pushed and I judge them?

A: You want to push them away.

Q: Yeah.

A: Well, I think what your ego is afraid of is joining with someone. As I mentioned I guess last night, that is an example of what the Course means when it says the ego then becomes vicious (T-9.VIII.2:9). When you begin to listen to the Holy Spirit—and one expression of that would be to join with people and not see yourself as separate from someone—the ego becomes frightened. And the ego says to you, "If you keep up this joining stuff, God is going to get you." The part of you that identifies with the ego says, "Oh, yeah, that's right, I forgot." And so quickly what you need is a defense against love. Well, what is a good defense against love? Anger. Finding fault. So instead of letting yourself draw close to someone, you push the person away. And anger of course is a very popular way of doing that. What you do when that happens is say, "Oh, the same thing has happened again. I must have become afraid of love. What else is new?" And don't make a big deal about it.

Seesaw

Another participant talked about the experience of flipping back and forth between the ego and the Holy Spirit. At the times of the greatest ego attacks, it is helpful to remember the other times when joining was the reality. He asked Ken if it's okay to be flipping back and forth like that.

K: Not only is it okay, everybody is going to do that. When you no longer flip back and forth, that is the attainment of the real world. That is the very end of the Atonement process. And that takes a lot of hard work. And that takes a long time. In the six stages of "The Development of Trust" in the teacher's manual, the sixth stage is the attainment of the real world (M-4.A.8). He doesn't use that term, but that is what it is talking about. And when it discusses the fifth stage, it says you may stay here a very long time (M-4.A.7:7). Because what you are talking about is the total undoing and disidentification with the ego. Until that point is reached, we go back and forth all the time. And so I think what you do is say, "Oh, I am going back and forth." Which means there is a part of me that really wants the love of God and a part of me that is afraid of it, and I go back and forth. Just be aware of that. When the seesaw starts, say, "Oh, I am back on the seesaw again. It is very hard for me to stay in one place."

Q: It's very hard not to be judgmental when you are taking a step back and –

K: Well that's what you don't want to do. That is why I quoted that line. Let me even show you where it is so you can underline it in your book. It's on page 383 in the text, the end of the first paragraph. And Jesus says:

(T-18.V.1:5-6) Put yourself not in charge of this, [not in charge of the plan] **for you cannot distinguish between advance and retreat. Some of your greatest advances you have judged as failures, and some of your deepest retreats you have evaluated as success.**

This is Jesus' kind way of saying that we don't know which end is up. (Laughter) So when you are tempted to judge yourself, say, "Oh, I am tempted to judge myself which means it is my ego doing a number on myself again." Because all of your judgments about yourself, just as all of your judgments about anybody else, are all based on form. And we know already that all of form is illusory. Form in and of itself has no meaning whatsoever. It is the meaning or the purpose that our mind gives it.

The Content of Chaos

Q: Is our preoccupation with law and order the ego's attempt to hold everything together?

A: Absolutely. Yes. Yes, because one way of understanding that from a psychological point of view is that the ego's basic thought is a disordered thought, as the Course explains at one point (T-5.V.7). It's disordered because it has stolen from God. God is the perfect Order. The ego itself is a disordered thought. What it tries to do is hide the content of the lack of order and the chaos that is really what it is. That is why the laws of chaos are the laws of the ego (T-23.II). The whole thing is absurd and insane.

The ego hides the content and miscreates a world in which there is law and order. So the planets seem to follow a certain order. And we have laws. We have laws of planetary motion. We have laws of gravity. We have this law and that law. And then we have laws that govern our society, all of which is the magical hope that by containing the form and having order in the form, I am going to have order in my thought.

And again, it is the ego's attempt to use form to contain and conceal what the content is. It never wants us to look at the content. We can say that the whole Course is about having us look at the content, without guilt, without fear, without a sense of sin. Simply look at the content with the Holy Spirit's love next to us and say, "Isn't that silly."

The Voice of the Ego

The next question had to do with the notion of conscience. A questioner commented that we think we can be listening to the voice of conscience, but conscience can be of the ego as well.

K: Not *can* be of the ego; it *is* of the ego.

Q: Always?

K: Well, conscience is guilt. Conscience is saying that there is something you shall not do or should not do or better not do, or should do. All of which is based upon criteria that are external. Good boys and girls don't do this. Or good boys and girls only do this, or whatever. Conscience really is the voice of the ego. There is nothing in the Course that can be taken as a guide for behavior. We talk about conscience, we are talking about behavior. You do something or you don't do something. This is right; this is wrong. There is no right and there is no wrong in the Course. All that there is, is there is guilt and forgiveness. Guilt will make us unhappy and forgiveness will make us happy. But there is no morality of saying there is something right or wrong. The only thing that the Course is against is guilt. And again, not because it is real or it is immoral or unethical, but simply because it won't make us happy.

The Ego Speaks First

Ken was asked to clarify the idea that the ego speaks first and is wrong. That seems to conflict a little with the idea of trusting one's own intuition.

K: When the Course says the ego speaks first and is wrong, it doesn't mean that when you meditate or pray, the first voice you hear will be the ego. What it means is that the ego speaks first in the sense of that it believes in separation. You would not have the need to pray or ask the Holy Spirit for help or to meditate unless you first believed you were separate. And unless you first believed you were a body. The Course explains how the ego always speaks first and the Holy Spirit is the answer to it. So again, the ego speaking first means that the very fact that you believe you have a body that has to meditate and pray and ask for help from the Holy Spirit, is the ego.

Then the answer I hear while I am meditating is from the Holy Spirit?

K: Well, that's up to you. It can be the Holy Spirit. If you have not let go of your guilt and your anger and your investment in being right, then the voice that you hear—and voice, doesn't mean necessarily hearing a voice. It can be an intuition or feeling. But the voice that you will hear *must* be your ego. If, however, you've let go of the interference or sufficiently let go of the interference, then the Voice that you hear will be the Holy Spirit. But it doesn't mean that the first voice you are going to hear is going to be the ego's.

Comforting Others

Ken was asked whether it is a form of hypocrisy to go to a funeral home and want to comfort grieving friends and family while at the same time trying to uphold what the Course says about death and mourning.

K: It is not hypocrisy if your purpose is to be loving. In the teacher's manual, when it talks about the ten characteristics of God's teachers, one of them is honesty—in fact, I think it's number two (M-4,II). The definition of honesty has nothing to do with behavior or what you do, what is right or wrong, what is honest or not honest on that level. The definition that is used is that your behavior, or what you do, is consistent with what you think.

If you go to a funeral and you are going as a teacher of God—in other words, that you have really learned this—then your goal is to be loving and peaceful. And to be a manifestation of that love and peace. That is the thought. Obviously, you can't be loving and peaceful if you separate yourself out from other people. The way that you would be loving and peaceful is to act and speak like everybody else. You say all the socially appropriate words. "I am very sorry to hear about your loss."

Whatever. You bring flowers or you send a card or, you know, you do all the things that "normal" people do.

Q: There is no loss.

K: No, there is no loss. But that love must be expressed in the form that people can accept. What makes you honest by saying, "I am sorry to hear about your loss" is not that you believe in the loss, but because that is your way of joining with someone who believes there is a loss. You join with them on the level of form, but with a different content. There is a consistency because of the purpose between what you think and what you do. At that point, then, there is no hypocrisy.

Q: Isn't that continuing to make the illusion real, though?

K: It depends on how you define the illusion. If you define the illusion as being the belief in separation, then my joining with you in the form in which you can accept my joining with you, is undoing that illusion. It isn't making it real. If I come into a funeral with this holy book in my hand, and I say "There is no death because Jesus says it in this book, and what are you so upset about?" clearly what I am doing is separating myself out from everybody.

I am joining with you on the illusion of form, because I am teaching you the truth of the content. Let me actually read the end of page 24, because that is really expresses it very well. I referred to it before.

(T-2.IV.5) The value of the Atonement does not lie in the manner in which it is expressed. In fact, if it is used truly, it will inevitably be expressed in whatever way is most helpful to the receiver. [The content of the Atonement is constant, but the form (the way it is expressed) would be what is helpful to you.] **This means that a miracle, to attain its full efficacy, must be expressed in a language that the recipient can understand without fear.** [If you are too afraid of the truth, that there is no death, which obviously you would be if you are grieving over the loss of a body, then to come in and say that the holy word of Jesus says there is no death, is going to terrify you. That is not going to help.] **This does not necessarily mean that this is the highest level of communication of which he is capable. It does mean, however, that it is the highest level of communication of which he is capable now. The whole aim of the miracle is to raise the level of communication, not to lower it by increasing fear.** [So speaking the form of truth may not be helpful.]

Q: So the idea of God calling me to be a certain someone or move some place, go to school or whatever, that's not –

K: No. The idea that God calls us or tells us to do certain things, which clearly is our experience many, many times—is not what really happens. Our experience is that it happens, just as our experience is that the sun rises and sets. And certainly it would be silly to deny that experience. But the truth is that love simply is there, and it is abstract. The Course says in one lesson how the natural condition of the mind is abstract (W.pI.161.2:1). The condition of the mind that is natural is love. And that is abstract; it is not specific.

So strictly speaking, God doesn't tell us what to do. What happens when we get our ego distortions out of the way, again, as I explained earlier, the love comes through us. And then it will take whatever form is the most helpful for us. Our experience is, just as the experience of the sun rising and setting, that the Holy Spirit or Jesus or God told me what to do. In reality, His love just came through my mind and took the form in which I needed to learn, in the way that I can accept His love.

Made in United States
North Haven, CT
30 May 2023

37152633R00096